UNBELIEVABLE

UNBELIEVABLE

From My Childhood Dreams
To Winning Olympic Gold

JESSICA
ENNIS

with Rick Broadbent

HODDER

First published in Great Britain in 2012 by Hodder & Stoughton
An Hachette UK company

First published in paperback in 2013
1

A CIP catalogue record for this title is available from the British Library

ISBN 978 1 444 76863 3

Typeset by Palimpsest Book Production Limited, Falkirk, Stirlingshire
Printed and bound by Clays Ltd, St Ives plc

Hodder & Stoughton policy is to use papers that are natural, renewable
and recyclable products and made from wood grown in sustainable
forests. The logging and manufacturing processes are expected to
conform to the environmental regulations of the country of origin.

Hodder & Stoughton Ltd
338 Euston Road
London NW1 3BH

www.hodder.co.uk

To Team Ennis, my family, friends and Andy.
The people who never stopped believing in me,
who inspired me and who have dedicated so much
of their time to making my dreams become a reality.

Contents

	Acknowledgements	ix
	Photographic Acknowledgements	xi
	Prologue – One Shot	1
1	A load of old tripe	5
2	The reluctant athlete	19
3	Tadpole	37
4	The odd couple	55
5	China girl	71
6	Open when champion	97
7	Reigning in Spain	119
8	The big time	135
9	The wheels come off	151
10	Dying to win	169
11	Trials and tribulations	187
12	Countdown	199

13	Eighty Thousand Friends	211
14	Aftermath	231
	Career Statistics	243
	Index	271

Acknowledgements

I have so many people to thank and I am so grateful to all those people for their help and support along the road to my Olympic gold, and if you are not mentioned in this book, you will know who you are and the part you played.

Above all I would like to thank my parents, Alison and Vinnie, and my sister, Carmel, for all their love and support. And of course I could not forget Grandad and Grandma, who are amongst my biggest fans, and Uncle Terry! I couldn't have done it without you.

Also a big thank you to all of my good friends who have helped keep my feet on the ground and love me for who I am.

Chell – what can I say – you have done a great job, always believed in me and made me laugh and cry along the way.

To the rest of Team Ennis – Mick, Bricey, Derry, Ali, Steve and everyone else who gave me their time and commitment on the performance side.

And Jane and Suzi who looked after me away from the track helping me balance my other commitments. To my sponsors who helped me both on the track and off – thank you.

Thanks to Roddy Bloomfield and Sarah Hammond at Hodder & Stoughton for helping bring this book together, as well as Eleni Lawrence, Lucy Zilberkweit, Laura Del Vescovo and Alasdair Oliver.

And to Rick Broadbent for his support over the years and for helping me tell my story, and to Graham Hughes for capturing my story of the past four years in pictures.

Finally, to Andy who has truly been the one who has held my hand through the last eight years and whose support, love and advice has been invaluable.

Oh and how could I forget Myla, my labrador, who has been the best distraction when I most needed it.

Photographic Acknowledgements

The author and publisher would like to thank the following for permission to reproduce photographs:

Mark Dadswell/Getty Images, Stu Forster/Getty Images, Dean Mouhtaropoulos/Getty Images, Dieter Nagl/AFP/Getty Images, Sheffield Star/Ross Parry Sindication, Michael Steele/ Getty Images, John Stillwell/PA Archive/Press Association Images.

All other photographs are from private collections.

Prologue

ONE SHOT

This is the day that I have dreamt about for years. This has been what all that dying on the side of a track has been about. This is the end of the raging pain. This is my one opportunity. My one shot. Walking into this arena is an assault on the senses – the purple and green and red, the crescendo of noise and the haze at the end of the straight where the Olympic flame is burning bright. This is it. This is my chance. I cannot help thinking that if it goes wrong I will never get this opportunity again. I might make another Olympics, but it won't be at home and I won't be touted as the face of the Games again. This combination of circumstances will never arise again. It is my first time and my last chance. Finally I realize just how big and scary the Olympic Games are. I follow the other girls to the start and we get into our blocks. It's like that Eminem song goes: one opportunity to seize everything you want. Will I capture the moment or let it slip?

It has taken me sixteen years to get here. Now I have seven events and two days to make it worthwhile. There have been countless times when I have wondered if it would happen. I have been down, broken and almost out, but I have dragged myself back from the brink. Part of me wonders how this has happened. I am just an ordinary girl from a run-of-the-mill street in Sheffield and yet I have been plucked out of that normality and plunged into this melting pot of hopes and dreams and fierce competition. It is what I have wanted when I have been training every day, but it is frightening.

I feel adrenaline, excitement and fear. I have lost my crowns in the last year and there are bigger, stronger girls ready to push me around. Tatyana Chernova is the world champion. Nataliya Dobrynska is the Olympic champion. I have no titles, just one shot. We crouch and the roar drops to total silence. It is that special moment of bated breath and possibility. And then suddenly, in those seconds before the gun, I feel a strange calmness wash over me and I am ready. It is now or never.

1

A LOAD OF
OLD TRIPE

I am crying. I am a Sheffield schoolgirl writing in her diary about the bullies awaiting me tomorrow. They stand menacingly by the gates and lurk unseen in my head, mocking my size and status. They make a small girl shrink, and I feel insecure and frightened. I pour the feelings out into words on the page, as if exposing them in some way will help, but nobody sees my diary. It is kept in my room as a hidden tale of hurt.

Fast forward two decades and I am crying again. I am standing in a cavernous arena in London. Suddenly, the pain and suffering and frustration give way to a flood of overwhelming emotion. In the middle of this enormous arena I feel smaller than ever, but I puff out my chest, look to the flag and stand tall. It has been a long and winding road from the streets of Sheffield to the tunnel that feeds into the Olympic Stadium like an artery.

I am Jessica Ennis. I have been called many things, from tadpole to poster girl, but I have had to fight to make that progression. I smile and am polite and so people think it comes easily, but it doesn't. I am not one of those athletes who slap their thighs and snarl before a competition, but there is a competitive animal inside, waiting to get out and fight for survival and recognition. Cover shoots and billboards are nice, but they are nothing without the work and I have left blood, sweat and tears on tracks all over the world. It is an age where young people are fed ideas of quick-fix fame and instant celebrity, but the tears mean more if the journey is hard. So I don't cry crocodile tears; I cry the real stuff.

I was a scrawny baby. That is no surprise. I have spent a lot of my life dealing with remarks about my size, both flippant and more calculated, so it was fitting that I weighed just 6 lb 8 oz when I was born in Nether Edge Hospital in Sheffield. The hospital used to be a workhouse for the Sheffield poor and much of it has now been turned into flats, with only a mental health unit surviving, but it was still flourishing when I arrived on 28 January 1986.

My mum and dad had not known each other very long before they had me. They took me back to Nether Edge, a mixed area where good bits nestled against mean streets, and I shared our house with chickens, cats, dogs and the parrot that my dad had felt sorry for when he saw it in a shop window one day.

My dad, Vinnie, was born in 1951 and is fourteen years older than my mum, Alison. He moved here from Jamaica in 1963, when he was twelve, following his parents who had emigrated looking for employment two years earlier. They were hard times for him. He was dealing with the emotional upheaval of leaving the Caribbean for England, and soon after found himself living with his grandparents when his mum and dad went to the USA. It is hard to imagine that happening now, but they were different times and my grandparents had to follow the work. It meant Dad and his brother, Uncle Danny, stayed here and had to deal with a new life without their parents to turn to for help.

My dad still misses Jamaica, but this is his home now and has been for most of his life. Occasionally, he will drift back in time and talk about how deeply miserable he was when he arrived, with the beaches and blue skies replaced by an unremitting greyness. 'Everything was dull and cold,' he says. The 1960s was also an era when racism was more prevalent. He does not talk about that side of his life much, but I know he must have gone through some bad times, and he has mentioned how he once went to buy a house, only for the owner to decide he did not fancy the idea of selling to a black man.

I think it may have been a shock for my grandparents, too, when he started going out with Mum after meeting her in a Sheffield pub in 1984. Mum was a rebel, a wild child, all naughtiness and dyed pink hair. When she was fourteen, she collected what money she had and went to stay overnight at a friend's house. Unbeknown to my grandparents, they had a grand plan and made their way to the coast where they took a ferry to France and stayed there until the cash ran out. It is that streak which makes her say to me sometimes: 'I'm sure you are adopted.' We are similar in lots of ways, but she was a troublemaker.

She was born in 1965 in Derbyshire and brought up in the countryside there with her brother Richard. Although she and Dad both hailed from farming back-grounds, the differences will initially have been far more obvious to my grandparents. Here was my mum, already a handful and difficult to contain, and now there was Dad, too, not only an older man but also a black one. Living out in the country, where the pace of change is slower, it must have been an eye-opener for them, although as soon as they got to know Dad, they warmed to him, and now they love him as much as they do Mum.

Mum's adventurous nature meant she wanted to get away from the country as quickly as possible. It also might have had something to do with my parents never getting married. As time went on, they just didn't see the need.

We moved houses a few times because money was tight and we downsized. Then Mum got pregnant again in 1988 and I remember us sitting on a bare living-room floor, her with a big bump, rolling a ball back and forth as Dad helped the removal men drag the furniture into our new home on Highfield Place, the place where I would spend most of my childhood.

My dad made his living from painting and decorating. He was self-employed and later fitted work around taking care of me and my sister. I have a vivid memory of me and Dad painting the walls of the bathroom for when Mum came home from hospital. Then I was taken to my grandparents while Dad went to be with Mum. The call finally came through that I had a sister and they were naming her Carmel. I was thrilled. When they brought this new baby back I was like any toddler, treating her as a personal plaything and always wanting to hold her, but as time went on and I realized I was not the centre of undivided attention, as I had been for the past three years, the relationship changed, gradually deteriorating into a teenage war zone.

My dad is a warm, lovely man and Carmel and I were definitely daddy's girls, but he was strict too. If we ever did anything wrong then we would make sure we did it when he was out. Both of us were smacked by our parents but, to be fair, we probably deserved it, and we had it a lot easier than some of our friends, one of whom was periodically beaten with a wooden spoon. I think parental discipline is very important, as long as you understand the reasoning behind it, and as long as it goes hand in hand with parental love.

The main source of problems in our house was sibling squabbling. Carmel would steal my clothes and that was enough to light the touchpaper. Once I knew that she had taken a top of mine. I confronted her, she denied it and then I went through her wardrobe and found it scrunched up at the bottom. It sounds insignificant, but nothing is insignificant when you are that young and I went mad.

I gave as good as I got, though, and was far from blameless. My biggest night of shame came when we were still sharing a room. I set the alarm clock and got up in the middle of the night.

'What are you doing?' Carmel asked sleepily.

'Oh, me and Mum are going on holiday,' I replied nonchalantly.

'Can I come?'

'No, it's just me and Mum,' I said as I put clothes into a suitcase. Of course, we were not going anywhere and I just wanted to upset her. I feel terrible about that now, but it hints at the nature of our relationship then. We did have plenty of good times, but it often ended in further tears and a sour atmosphere. It was like that when we were jumping across the divide from her bed to mine, and we were both a mix of smiles and fun, right up until the point when she went straight into the wall, her nose exploded and she was left covered in blood. Eventually, as I got older, it was decided I needed more space and so I got the attic room and moved out.

It was hard for Mum because she was working in residential rehab and could be on a shift pattern that meant we got home from school as she was leaving for work. It meant we spent a lot of time with Dad, who was self-employed and able to be flexible. I think his background, being separated from his own parents by thousands of miles, was a contributory factor in that. He did not want us to be another splintered family. We are very close, even if the only photograph I ever had on my bedside table when I was a child was not of my parents or my sister, but of Will Smith, the actor. I later had the opportunity to appear with him on *The Graham Norton Show* just before the Olympics, but had to decline due to training – I am and always will be gutted.

Even though he had been living in England for so long, Dad's Jamaican roots often influenced our daily life. That was certainly the case in the kitchen. He cooked a lot and much of it had a Caribbean flavour. So he would cook ackee and saltfish, the national dish, or an array of exotic fare like curried goat and pig's trotters. Mum would cook more conventional dishes, but would always make sure that we were eating healthily and not living on convenience food.

A particular favourite of Dad's was kippers. I would get this nauseous sensation when I smelt these waves of kipper essence wafting up the stairs and through every part of the house. There was no escape. He would clean the grill pan, but the flavour infused everything and so I would find myself eating fishy toast. To this day, I still don't like fish as a result of being scarred for life by Dad's kippers.

By contrast, Mum says the secret of my success is a load of old tripe. Literally. Dad used to have it with onions every weekend, and I was weaned on liquidized tripe and milk. A quarter of a century later I appeared on *A League of Their Own*, a panel show with a sporting theme, and they had caught wind of my old diet. A pint of tripe was placed on the desk and the guests were dared to drink it. I shuddered and shied away from it, whereupon Andrew Flintoff, the former cricketer, picked it up, downed it, wiped his mouth with the back of his hand and declared: 'I've had worse.' He managed to spill some of it on me as he quaffed away and I revisited my childhood disgust.

Mum always says that I was a demanding child who was never satisfied and could create an argument anywhere. 'Once she'd done one drawing it would be, "Right, what's next?"' she recalled in an interview. 'I took her to nursery and, even before I'd left, she done all the activities and it would be, "I'm ready to come home now." She always needed entertaining. She was hard work until the age of three. She always wanted to do what she wanted and so, as a baby, she cried a lot. The very young years I found hardest. I thought it was because I was a bad mother.'

My mum also says that she thinks she may have passed

on the competitive gene. Dad was quite sporty and, like most Jamaican kids, did some sprinting, but Mum admits she is competitive on a petty scale. If my leg is hurting, her hip hurts more. Her cake will have to be better than my cake. They joke that I am adopted, but I am an individual mix of my parents' different personalities and cultures.

Even though we did not have a lot of money, and spent our childhoods dressed in clothes from charity shops and hand-me-downs, my parents never allowed us to feel that we were missing out. At Christmas our friends would often get lots of expensive presents, but we would have lots of little things instead. The thought counted more and I felt some parents were just trying to compensate for not being there. For us, Christmas was always a special time, whatever we had, which is why Dad got into such severe trouble one day when he left the wardrobe doors open and we saw all the presents lying there. Mum was furious as secrets were exposed, but for the most part we were a practical family wrapped up and bonded by circumstance. If we rarely went on holidays because of the finances, we did not mind, and when we did make it to Abersoch, in a cramped caravan, with our grandparents in tow, that was a bonus.

Mum had a friend called Michelle when we were little. She had two children, Libby and Eddie. Libby was Carmel's age and Eddie was two years older than me. We did a lot together as Mum was a firm believer in wearing out your children, so there would be lots of trips to the country in Michelle's undersized Fiat Panda, kids on knees, no seat belts, picnic in the back. I hated the walking, but I was six and hopelessly in love with Eddie.

He had long blond hair and was as cute as they come. 'We'll get married one day,' I'd think as we held hands. I have a vivid memory of writing lots of Valentine's Day cards to him, but then hiding them away and never sending them, undone by shyness.

My closest girlfriend was Charlotte. We met at infants and remained best friends through school, university, sport and adulthood. I would follow her around and do whatever she wanted to do. 'Don't be a sheep,' my mum would tell me, but I ignored her and joined the brass band, playing the trombone, not through any great love of music, but because Charlotte played the cornet. I also had a close friend, Lorna. Both of us had a fixation with the film *The Bodyguard*, and especially Whitney Houston. I was about twelve years old when I decided I would cut my hair like hers, so I began to hack away. The results were devastating, an uneven mess that was more like a crew cut. It was the worst hairstyle I'd had since I had a Mohican as a baby and Mum had to spend ages trying to make it right and consoling me.

In 1993 my parents sent me to Sharrow Junior School. In terms of academic results it was not the best, but Mum was keen for me to go somewhere that had a rich mix of races and cultures. I think she felt that was more important in those formative years. I now think that was a shrewd decision, because children can be unforgiving about differences, picking them out and using them as sticks to beat you with. I knew that because I was still the smallest in the class and I became more self-conscious about it as the years went by. Swimming was a particular ordeal, and in my mind now, I can still see this young, timid wisp standing by the side of a pool in her red swimming costume quaking with anxiety.

I was small and scraggy and that was when the bullying started. There were two girls who were really nasty to me. They did not hit me, but bullying can take on many forms and the abuse and name-calling hurt. The saying about sticks and stones breaking bones but words never hurting falls on deaf ears when you are a schoolkid in the throes of a verbal beating. At that age, girls can be almost paralysed by their self-consciousness, so each nasty little word cut deep wounds. I went home, cried and wrote in my diary. Perhaps it would be nice to say that one day I fought back and beat the bullies, but I didn't. It festered away and became a big thing in my life, leaving me wracked with fear about what they would say or do next.

It got to the point that I dreaded seeing them at school. And then we moved onto secondary school and

I found out that they were going there too. The dread got deeper. Later, I did tell my mum. 'They are only jealous of you,' she replied. But jealous of what? I could not understand it. I tried to deal with it myself, but that was impossible. I would rely on my diary and hope for the best, but that was not much of a defence against these scary girls who were dominating my thoughts. And then, around that time, my mum saw an advert for a summer sports camp at the Don Valley Stadium in Sheffield. It was my first taste of sport and it would be the first tentative step towards fighting back and getting my own quiet revenge on the bullies.

2

THE RELUCTANT ATHLETE

I was in a hurry. What can I do now? What can I draw next? When can we go home? I hurtled through everything at breakneck speed, fuelled by impatience and boredom. It was a lot for Mum to deal with. Her work was stressful and involved a lot of emotional investment. It is the same now that she is a manager for the Turning Point charity, working with those affected by drug and alcohol addiction. She has always been a caring person, but she was at her wits' end in the summer of 1996, so the Aviva Startrack camp was a godsend.

I went down with my sister Carmel, and our friends Libby and Eddie. I was anxious because there seemed to be hundreds of kids there, and I sat on the cold stone steps feeling nervous and insecure. The abiding memory of that first day now is the smell of the track. It is hard to describe, but it is special – not a sweaty staleness, but something unique to athletics. I dragged it in and never forgot it. Before long I was smitten. There was a range of coaches there, and we were split into different groups and spent two weeks trying all the different events. For someone prone to a short attention span, it was varied and fun. When the sun came out and baked the infield, there were water fights and a lot of laughs. This is when I made friends with Lorna and we were both completely hooked.

Carmel was less enthused. She sat on the steps at the Don Valley chatting to people; she didn't really care for the activities. She was always more social than sporting and, when she came to secondary school, would try anything to get out of PE lessons. I don't know how she managed it but she even convinced Mum to write her notes a few times to get her excused. I think it is important to stress that, while championing the merits of sport and an active lifestyle, you have to remember people are different. Not everyone likes sport. Some people hate it. Even I'm not that interested in watching it. I like doing it but I have never considered myself a sports nut and I don't have an evangelical belief in spreading the gospel, because it is all about finding what you like and want to do.

Carmel did not much care for school in general back then. We had gone to King Ecgbert's School in the little village of Dore in South Sheffield. Ecgbert was reputedly the first king of England and Dore was a much posher area, so it was a step up for us. The local school had a bad reputation and has since been knocked down, so it was a choice between King Ecgbert's and another. As far as I was concerned, there was no debate, because my good friend Charlotte was going to join her sister at King Ecgbert's and that sealed the deal. I started in September 1997. I was still terrified on the first day. I was not a confident child and almost froze when my dad asked me to go and get the paper from the corner shop one day.

'On my own?'

Dad barely looked at me. 'Yes, here's the money.'

He knew I needed to shed some of my inhibitions, but I still remember going to big school and being frightened. There were two buildings, Wessex and Mercia, separated by a changeover path, and as I was edging along it one day, I heard an older girl say: 'Oh, look at her, she's so tiny and cute.' That made me feel ten times worse.

Sport, though, was becoming an outlet for the insecurities and I found I was good at it. Mick Thompson and Andy Bull were two of the Startrack coaches who first thought there might be the semblance of some ability. They said they could just tell. You watch children running and they all do it in different ways, but some of them are fluid and natural. I won a free pair of trainers at the Startrack camp and came home enthusing about it. Grandad says that, after that, I was always asking him to time me in the garden. Andy, who went to the same school and later became my boyfriend, says he remembers me running between the Wessex and Mercia buildings, timing myself. I think he is exaggerating, but I had got the bug, and when in 1996 Mick asked me to start training at Don Valley once a week, I said yes.

I had tried other things. Charlotte played basketball and so I gave it a go too. We played for the Sheffield Hatters junior team, but I was rubbish. I also realized that I was not cut out for team games. There was a nice sense of camaraderie and I liked the fact we were all in it together, but I much preferred being in charge of my own destiny. When things go wrong in a team, you can always shift the blame onto someone else, but I thrived on the sense of responsibility and control. Perhaps it was being the first born, but I liked athletics from the start and did not want to do anything else.

Gradually, I became more popular. The two bullies were still there, but if I was talking to anyone going through something similar I would stress that things change quickly. It does not seem like it at the time, of course, with every week an endless agony of groundhog days, but it soon fades. I slowly made friends and the tide turned. The same girls who had bullied me now wanted to be my friends. It was all part of that whirlpool of hormones and petty jealousies that is part of being a young girl. Now I do not think they were inherently nasty people, but I know what I have done with my life and I think I am in a better position.

Sport helped me at school. It does not always work that way and you can be classed as a sport geek, but the teachers began to make more of a fuss. One of the teachers, Malcolm Rogers, is now an athletics official and he would say things like: 'It's three weeks until sports day, so make sure you all support Jessica.' By year seven, when I was eleven, the PE teachers, Chris Eccles and Rick Cotgreave, said they felt I could be something special. I was high-jumping well then, despite my size, and it was not long until I was out-jumping older boys and, naturally, they hated that; nobody likes being beaten by a girl. One boy would keep bugging me to race him. I would refuse. I was training twice a week at Don Valley now and in 1998 I joined the City of Sheffield Athletics Club. I figured that I was training on a proper track and taking it seriously, so why should I take a step down and take on some boy with a dented ego?

It probably didn't help Carmel, though. By the time she got to secondary school, the teachers would remind her of how well I was doing. 'Oh, so you're Jessica Ennis's sister, you must be good at sport.' She had no desire to be good at it, and we found ourselves on diverging paths, but school had not been a breeze for me either. It is a stressful time because all anyone wants to do at that age is fit in. I might have been high-jumping well, but I came home in year seven with my predicted grades and they were terrible – a raft of Es. Charlotte was the sort of girl who never needed to study hard and yet she would sail through, but I realized that day that I was different. I needed to work hard to get on. Something clicked. The competitive gene emerged. I had a need to be successful at everything I did and so I started to study hard as well.

Carmel was more like Mum. She was the rebel and could be a bit naughty. She had a tough time at school, with bullying beyond anything I had suffered. I wanted to help and gave the bullies a few stern looks and harsh words, but it was hard for her. Then she fell in with a group of friends I thought were dragging her down, but the thing with Carmel was she always saw the best in people, overlooking the negatives and finding the good. Nevertheless, it got to the stage where she refused to go to school. Dad had to drive her to the school gates and watch her walk through the door. He did not know that she would just wait until he had driven off and then walk out. It was tough for everyone because, as a parent, there is only so much that you can do.

I was glad I had athletics as a focus. I had the pair of cheap trainers I had won from the Startrack camp and began focusing on the sprints. Then I did the high jump. I liked the hurdles and Mick Thompson and Andy Bull said they were surprised at how well I took to such a technical event. In those days coaches moved around the varying groups at Don Valley and so I quickly ended up with Nicola Gautier.

I was in total awe of her. She would go on to become a world champion bobsleigh driver, but she was still a heptathlete back then. She was an animal in the way she was so aggressive in her approach to the hurdles and it made me wonder if I could ever succeed. I would watch her slap her thighs, growl, and go through the tics and tones that a lot of athletes use to fire themselves up; it made me feel lots of inner doubts.

Nicola was being coached by her future husband, Toni Minichiello, a bearlike man of Italian descent, and before long I was passed onto him. It was the start of a love-hate relationship that has caused me more tears, pain and ultimately joy than I could have ever dreaded or wished for. I was thirteen and utterly intimidated by this coach with the sharp tongue and fierce reputation. He was relatively new to being a coach then and, having eked out a fairly modest career as a decathlete, was looking for athletes. I remember him coming over and speaking to Mum and before you knew it we were a team, often disunited, often bickering, but with a combined desire to be better.

It did not always show. One day I went down to the Don Valley with Lorna and there was a free-for-all tug-of-war going on in the middle. We skipped down the steps and rushed to join in. There was a lot of laughing and joking and then a deep voice bellowed down from the stand.

'If you two are not going to come down here and train properly, then you are going to have to go.'

Toni was furious and I quivered a bit. I also thought, 'I don't know if I want to do this if it's going to be this serious. It's not the same thing I signed up to a year ago.'

It was scarcely the most glamorous of hobbies either. We went to Grimsby once for a race, sharing a car and braving monsoon-like conditions to compete in a decrepit stadium. The rain was relentless and I stood there in my oversized, bright yellow City of Sheffield T-shirt, the wind billowing against it and exaggerating its bagginess. It was grim, and Mum shivered in the shadows, no doubt shaking her head internally and wondering what on earth we were doing. But there was something inside me. I was fixated on the other girls, obsessing at how big and good they were, looking down at myself running, spidery limbs going everywhere, confidence low, but I emerged from it all wanting to do it again.

I still had a social life at that time, but juggling the two would become increasingly hard as I got better and the demands grew tougher. At first I was just one of the girls, meeting up in Sheffield city centre outside HMV and going for a McDonald's, but Saturdays slowly became dominated by athletics.

In July 1999, when I was thirteen, I went to Bury St Edmunds for the English Schools Championships. That was a huge deal. For me, at that stage, it was like the

Olympics. It entailed a six-hour coach ride with the whole South Yorkshire team and two days away from home. I was crippled with nerves on the way and then got heat-stroke. I felt a bit like a fish out of water, frying in the sun and out of my comfort zone. I came tenth in the high jump with a mighty leap of 1.55 metres. Soon after, Toni, whom everyone called Chell, put me in for the English Schools pentathlon held at The Embankment athletics track in Peterborough. It was another unspectacular performance. I finished fifteenth and the record does not make pretty reading. My shot put was 6.75 metres, my long jump a mere 4.38 metres and I rounded things off with a pedestrian 800 metres completed in an agonizingly drawn-out 2 minutes 54 seconds. Part of you thinks that everything will always go right and that you will win everything. It is that resilient optimism that is more evident as a child. But you live in the moment too, and so when the moment is bad, your emotions are rawer.

Things did improve at the English Schools competitions over the next few years. The following summer, in 2000, I won the junior girls' high-jump title with 1.70 metres. The next year I was second in the intermediate girls to Emma Perkins with a jump of 1.71. Another year on, in 2002, and I was first and Emma Perkins was second and both of us jumped 1.80 metres. Chell usually entered me for the combined events too – first the pentathlon and then the heptathlon. In 2001, I had improved to second place, finishing behind Phyllis Agbo. My shot put was up to 8.59 metres and my 800 metres was down to 2 minutes 29 seconds. Phyllis was better than me, though, and the one most people would have tipped to go on. I was second to her again in 2002, this time in the heptathlon, and our roles seemed to have been set.

When I was thirteen I suffered my first major injury, although it wasn't on the track. A friend was hosting a fancy dress party and a group of us were getting ready at my house. My parents were out and there was plenty of banter and frivolity. I had decided to go dressed as Pippi Longstocking, the character from the children's books who is renowned for superhuman strength and her appealing way of mocking condescending adults. I heard some boys coming past and so, as a prank, I decided to lock a couple of girls outside so that they would be embarrassed. The joke backfired when, after the routine screams, one of them, Rosie Manning, shoved the plate glass of the door. It shattered everywhere and the shards dug into me, slashing my arm. Rosie's wrists were a mess and, amid the blood and tears and shrieks, I remember thinking with trepidation about how much trouble I was going to be in.

A neighbour took us to hospital and I felt a dark wave rushing through my body and I came close to passing out. When my parents arrived at the hospital, I was in tears. I said I was sorry about the door, but of course they did not care about that. 'Don't worry, don't worry,' my dad said. It sounds sick I know, but I had always wanted a scar, so I was quite pleased with the telltale mark that I still have on my arm. Little did I know that more serious injuries and deeper mental scars lay ahead.

I was intimidated by everyone at the track at first and it took me a few years before I stopped being scared of Chell too. He just had a very blunt way and it often made me upset. I was sensitive and he did not realize that. Sometimes he still says things and I think, 'You can't say that,' but perhaps it is his way of dragging the best out of us all.

The group evolved and people gradually drifted away. It happens, especially with girls. They get to the ages of fifteen and sixteen and the temptations of teenage life seem more pleasurable than slogging your guts out on a wet and windy track while receiving barbs and brickbats. We still had a great group, though, and I became really good friends with Hannah, who was a couple of years older. It was still a difficult situation as quite a few of the girls were older and started going out a lot. There were lots of parties and my friends would get exasperated with me.

'Oh, come on, you're always training,' they would say.

I was, and it was hard, but I already knew, at the age of fifteen, that I wanted to be an athlete. I had fledgling ideas of being a chef or a journalist, but deep down I knew that, for some reason, I wanted this.

'All I want to do is be on top of the podium,' I told my parents.

'You will be,' they said.

'But when?'

'One day. Soon.'

By the sixth form I was training every night and competing at weekends. It was relentless. I have kept my friends from school, but we were doing different things then. My friends generally had more money than me too, either because their parents would help or because they could go out and get part-time jobs, but I struggled for time and money. It was my choice to do this, but I also felt as if I was missing out.

It was around that time when Chell began calling me 'the reluctant athlete', and there were plenty of times when I just did not want to go training. There were other times, after more hard words had left me a crumpled wreck crying in my room, that my dad decided he was going to go down to the track and have a word with this coach.

'Don't,' I said. 'It will only make it worse.'

My parents have never really been ones to intervene. They are the antithesis of the pushy parents so prevalent around sport and schools. Chell and I would go to the English Schools competitions and be amazed at the pressure heaped on the kids by their parents. Many would scream at them and berate them if the times did not add up. It was sad to see and made you understand why so many dropped out. In fairness to Chell, he always had a long-term plan. Many coaches want the reflected glory of their athletes' trophies and titles, but Chell was never like that. He was in it for the long haul and said that the plan was not to make me a great junior but a great senior. For someone with an impatient streak, that was hard to grasp, but I am glad that I did not have a coach or parents living out their dreams through me and driving me headlong towards burn-out.

The one time my dad did intervene was when a girl at school said something racist about me to my friend Charlotte. She told me, I told my parents, and Dad went round to the girl's house and shouted at her on the doorstep. It probably unearthed old wounds for him, but it is the only time I have ever encountered anything like that. I never consider the colour of my parents and I was amazed when I saw on Twitter that someone had posted a message: 'Jessica Ennis's dad is black – I can't believe it.' What couldn't they believe?

Normally, though, Dad was the sort to offer gentle shoves rather than full-blooded pushes. My grandad, Rod Powell, also played his part in teasing the reluctant athlete back into the fray. He would offer me incentives, perhaps five pounds, if I got a personal best at this competition or won there. He had been an active sportsman himself, and played football and tennis into his sixties, so he loved the fact I was doing so much, albeit that interest probably helped alienate Carmel all the more as I received both cash and attention.

But during the sixth form I did try to do everything. My parents are quite liberal and would allow me to go out as long as I was in by midnight. A couple of other friends from school, Georgina and Lauren, had parents who were much stricter and did not like them going out at all. However, one time I remember Lauren and I both sneaked out and headed to a bar. Unfortunately for me, Eddie was in the bar and he told his mum, who told mine. I was undone by my first love. Mum was mad but not crazy, fixing me with guilt-inducing eyes and saying: 'Have you got something to tell me?'

The turning point came when I was sixteen. I went to a friend's house party and there was a lot of alcohol. Someone spilt drinks and someone else tried to clean the carpet by pouring bleach all over it. I drank too much and crashed out. The next morning Grandad arrived, as planned, to take me to my athletics competition. I pulled the pillow over my head and tried to ignore the crushing headache. I really did not want to go, but I knew I had no choice. I got out of the house and was sick before I even got into Grandad's car. We drove to the track at Woodburn Road in silence and I could tell how annoyed he was. I got changed and then I was sick again. I saw Chell and tried to hide my condition from him. It was a horrible feeling and I realized I could not do both now. I had to choose between athletics and a normal teenage, party-going lifestyle. It was the day I decided the sacrifice was worth it. There would be time for partying later on and I did not want to look back with regrets. From that day on I would not even go out before a big day's training, because I knew that I would not get the maximum from the session. I swallowed my pride, walked out onto the track at Woodburn Road, somehow jumped a personal best in the high jump, and that was the end of the reluctant athlete.

3

TADPOLE

was improving year on year and I found that exciting. I was not imagining Olympic Games and global glory, but the slow rise through the junior ranks was enough to keep me interested.

I managed to trade my first hand-me-down spikes from Nicola Gautier for a new pair from the Keep On Running shop near the Don Valley. That was a big deal, but I needed them because it was growing more serious by the year. In truth, it always had been, thanks to Chell's approach and my desire. So I started competing abroad, getting picked to represent Great Britain in a four-team challenge in Switzerland when I was sixteen. The heptathlon was becoming my focus now and I liked it for the variety and the challenge of trying to do seven events. I scored 5194 points and came second. It was a nerve-wracking experience being away from home, but I was managing to bottle the fears. I still felt intimidated when I saw the bigger, more muscle-clad girls at the start, but I was measuring myself against myself, previous scores from previous years, and felt happier doing that. The strange thing about athletics is that you are up against rivals, but have little power to influence what they do. There can be a good deal of mind games and posturing, but essentially it's an individual event, you against yourself, your best versus your inner fears.

It was around that time that I got my first Lottery funding. It was £500 a year and was a big deal to me. Some athletes blew it on stupid things, but I needed it, not least for physio. Chell was always keen on getting me checked out and I was young when I first started seeing Alison Rose, a physiotherapist who would spend most of 2004 patching Kelly Holmes together and preventing her coming apart at raggedy seams as she ground her way to two gold medals. Ali would go on to be a key part of a group that we would christen Team Ennis, and would be a confidante and friend when things reached breaking point.

Initially, I felt differently, and could not understand how this physio treatment was going to be good for me. She hurt me so much, with violent use of elbows, and I did not want to go back, only to be told I needed it by Chell. He was right, too – one of the few times I would admit as much.

My first big event abroad was the World Youth

Championships in Sherbrooke, Canada, in July 2003. Mum came to watch with my grandparents because they had family out there, and so they went to visit them. The biggest competition I had been to so far was the English Schools, so it was a huge step up. I did not notice the tall, gangly Jamaican who won the 200 metres in a championship record time and who went by the name of Usain Bolt, and was just thinking about my own performance. The heptathlon takes place over two days, with four events on day one – the hurdles, high jump, shot put and 200 metres, and three on day two – long jump, javelin and 800 metres; it was in Canada where it became blindingly obvious that I had a good day and a bad one.

I started well but faded to fifth place on day two. One of the top girls came up to me afterwards.

'You should have won it.' she said.

I smiled and thanked her, but I knew I was not going to get anywhere until I sorted out the second day. It had ruined everything. It was the same the following year when I went to the World Junior Championships in Grosseto in Italy and again suffered a second-day slump into eighth place. I grew frustrated because I had tasted the thrill of being near the top, only for it to be ripped away by weaker events. I decided I had to go away and work harder on day two.

Things were still not great between me and Carmel at home. I only met my paternal grandad twice and when

I was a teenager he fell ill and Dad flew to America. He was dying, and Dad was really cut up about it, because he wished that they had remained a closer family. While he was away, things deteriorated and I revised for my GCSEs to the backbeat of slammed doors and raised voices.

I had the chance to go to America myself in 2004 when it came to choosing universities. I had been offered the possibility of going to East Carolina University on a scholarship. I was surprised because all I had done was go to the World Juniors and World Youths by that point, and I did not understand how they even knew about me, but I thought I should take a look and so Mum and I flew out there. They invited some of the track girls around to give us the hard sell. They were exactly how I imagined Americans: getting pizzas in, being hugely enthusiastic and gushing, 'Oh my God, it's so amazing.' I felt that they were so different to the British and in many ways the whole set-up seemed dated. It was just so unlike everything I was used to and, although the facilities were great and Coach Kaiser sends me messages still, I thought it would all feel odd and unsettling. When one of the girls said, 'And once a month we get to party', I decided that was it.

Everybody was pleased. Chell had said to me: 'If you go anywhere else, it's not going to work.' I knew I had a great set-up and that he was a great coach doing amazing things for me, but it was an important stage of my life and, having been with Chell since 1999, I now wanted to assess my options.

But with Chell whispering in my ear and Carolina a fading memory, I chose to go to Sheffield University. It might sound parochial, but I love this place. I was made in Sheffield and, from the Don Valley Stadium, where the smell of the track can still transport me back to being a ten-year-old girl sitting on the concrete steps, to the Peace Gardens, where I would one day be treated to a civic reception, I feel this city is part of me.

I had also started seeing Andy that year. He went to King Ecgbert's like me, but was three years older, which makes a big difference at that age. He had gone out with my friend Charlotte's big sister and thought of me as Little Jess. We met on a night out in a club called Republic. He says I chased him around the dance floor, but I really didn't. We talked and exchanged numbers. A few days later I went for a drink with my friend Georgina and she persuaded me to text him and invite him to join us. He came along and I liked him. We went out on our own soon afterwards and, although I didn't want to tempt fate, I knew from the start that I was going to fall deeply in love with him. He was on his year out from doing a construction management degree and I thought it was healthy that he was not into athletics. There are a few couples within the sport, but I like a release, and when I see my friends I want to know how they are doing.

I stayed put in Sheffield, but I still wanted to leave home. I knew that halls of residence would be far too distracting and could derail my ambitions, so I moved in with Hannah, one of the other girls in Chell's group.

I was still struggling for money. My great uncle, Grandad's sister's husband, Uncle Terry, realized that and helped me out by buying me a car, which meant I could get to training and competitions, without having to rely on my parents and Grandad. I took out a student loan, but that was going on tuition fees and books, so I got a job on the reception at the Virgin Active gym. I hated it as much as my previous part-time jobs. There had been an ill-fated spell working as a waitress in a city hotel. That ended badly when I spilt gravy all over one of the guests. The chefs also persuaded me that I had made the right choice in not pursuing that as a career as they were rude and horrible, terrorizing the waitresses and never accepting that anything could ever be their fault. I also took a job at Pizza Hut. Charlotte and I went in to pick up a pizza one day and saw some job openings and thought it would be fun so we applied. Alas, it was not quite as much fun as we had thought as we greased pans, took phone orders and tried to ignore some of the men who worked there and were a bit strange. The upside was we did get free pizzas after every shift. It was some time before I realized this might not be ideal when trying to pursue an athletics career.

I had got some money together, although some of it

was for one last blow-out before university, and so in the summer of 2004 six of us went to San Antonio, the party capital of Ibiza, before we parted ways. Andy was worried about me going but had no need to be, even though it quickly descended into carnage and a series of rows so bad that I honestly did not think any of us would ever speak to each other again. However, amid the strops and the foam that engulfed the dance floor at Pacha, there was one significant fact about that holiday that stuck in my memory. It came when I picked up a newspaper and saw a picture of Kelly Sotherton, the British heptathlete, receiving her bronze medal at the Athens Olympics which were taking place at the same time. Her coach, Charles van Commenee, had branded her a wimp and reduced her to tears for not getting the silver medal. I got ready for another night's clubbing and could not imagine that both of those people would have roles to play in my own Olympic journey.

I chose to study psychology. I was particularly interested in social psychology and how people reacted to one another. A number of famous studies captured my imagination. One of them was the controversial Milgram experiment where ordinary people believed they were giving huge electric shocks to innocent people. The theory was that people could be coerced into acting in appalling ways due to an unwavering belief in obedience. I found this fascinating, the idea that people could act against their natures due to external pressures, and I became interested in people's perceptions of psychological disorders. It is so easy to say to people 'snap out of it', without paying attention to the hardwiring of the brain and the biological side of things.

I did my dissertation on self-regulation. Broadly speaking, it is the idea that there is an area of the brain that self-regulates, but if, for example, you were on a diet, you would only have a certain amount of strength and willpower. The area becomes fatigued but you can train it. My tutor specialized in self-regulation in cricketers and it is an important area in sport, where repetition and visualization play important roles in success.

The psychology of sports is interesting and there are lots of issues that affect people. It is an elitist, cut-throat world and it is, inevitably, results-driven. That can lead to lots of pressure and even desperate measures. In athletics, eating disorders are not uncommon. I occasionally see people who I can tell are suffering, and I have heard lots of stories about long-distance runners suffering from bulimia and anorexia.

It is hard because in athletics there is a lot of pressure to look a certain way. That is why people need to be careful about the language they use. I was lucky in the sense that I have never had problems with my weight. I have always had a sweet tooth and big appetite, but my mum was skinny and so it is more down to genetics with me. However, the flip side of that is that you need to be quite muscly to be a heptathlete. When I started doing sessions in the gym I just did not want to be good at it. I would not push myself because I felt big muscles were unattractive and none of my friends at school had them. Many girls just do not want to stand out in their teenage years and, apart from when it came to athletics, I was the same.

Chell grew frustrated with this attitude, because he could see that I was not pushing myself.

'I don't want to lift this,' I would tell him.

'You've got to if you want to get better.'

'I don't know if I do then.'

As time wore on I realized Chell was right and that, if I wanted to be a successful, then I needed to do the gym sessions properly. My perspective changed. If I could be guaranteed to win an Olympic gold medal and had to have big muscles to do it, then of course I would, but as a teenage girl I was more self-conscious. I would not wear certain things and, to some extent, I am the same now and will usually cover my arms. I look at myself in the mirror and think I am a bit butch, but you get to a point where you finally understand that looks do not matter so much.

I was not a normal student and did not lead a normal student life. In my second year I competed in Cudworth and Turkey, Grimsby and Lithuania. The hurdles and the high jump were my best events, but I liked the variety of the heptathlon with its seven disciplines and numerous ways to foul up. In 2004 the press had damned us as the worst ever British team to go to the World Junior Championships. The medal count was terrible and we were really slated. That was my first taste of a negative media and it was quite hard, but in July 2005, aged nineteen, I went to Kaunas, the second biggest city in Lithuania, for the European Juniors.

Finally, it all came together. Everything went well for once and the work we had done on the second day paid off. I scored 5891 points to take the gold medal. The rain was cold and hard, but as I got the medal and heard the National Anthem piped through the stadium, flecked by a few hardy fans, I felt close to complete. I remembered the times I had told my dad that all I ever wanted to do was stand on the top of the podium. It was an intensely emotional experience, because it felt like it had taken so long to get there. The hotel was in the middle of the town and there was a lot going on, but I didn't go mad socially and was just happy with having achieved a goal.

I was taking athletics far more seriously than some other competitors at that age. As I have mentioned, the act of juggling a fledgling sporting career with a normal teenage life is nigh-on impossible and that trip to Lithuania showed it; one of the team let himself down and I have a bad memory of him throwing up over himself on the way back to the airport. In some ways you can understand it as it is the first time a lot of people have gone away from home, but it can get out of hand and you hear grisly stories of girls having their stomachs pumped. It can get messy.

But I had my head down now and felt I was making progress. A few weeks later, in August 2005, I went to Izmir in Turkey for the World Student Games. I added a few more points to my overall score and got 5910, enough for third place. The winner that day was a Ukrainian woman called Lyudmila Blonska who would also come to have a significant and slightly sinister part in my story.

It had been my breakthrough year. I really felt I was getting somewhere now and that there might be a career in it, although I never thought about money. Nobody gets into athletics for that and, if it does come, then that is just a nice by-product. I had some minimal funding and a student loan, but it was still hard to make ends meet and that Christmas I had no money to buy any presents. I was still scratching around but I was also scratching the itch, the nagging thought that I had to do this, and I felt content.

However, there was still a gulf in class between a top junior and a good senior. I went to the AAAs Championships in July 2005 and was third in the hurdles and joint sixth in the high jump. My wins were coming in meetings like the unspectacularly named Northern League Northern

Premier Division, and at places like Cleethorpes and Cudworth. It was hard to find any glamour in the sandpit at Grimsby either.

I was not a good university student. Not for the usual reasons of staying out late in the bar or sleeping in, but because I had to skip lectures to train. I always tried to catch up and the tutors were great, but it really got hard when I was picked to represent England at the Commonwealth Games in Melbourne in March 2006, a few months before my finals.

I was sharing a room with Julie Hollman, a heptathlete who had come fifth at the Commonwealth Games back in 2002, but the big stars of the combined events team were Dean Macey and Kelly Sotherton. Both had a lot of personality. Dean was a tattooed maverick from Canvey Island who preferred to talk about maggots and fishing than athletics, while Kelly had a habit of bluntly saying what she thought. She was always totally honest and the media, more used to platitudes and PR niceties, lapped it up.

The Commonwealth Games were a huge deal to me because it was my first major senior event. At the time my best score was 5910, but in global terms that was the froth of small beer. Carolina Klüft, the Swede who bestrode the event, had clocked 6952 points to win the Olympic gold in Athens, with Kelly scoring 6424 points in third. That seemed a different world.

'Just go out there and enjoy it,' Chell said. 'You've done the work.'

I did enjoy it but was a mess of nerves too. Chell could not afford to travel to the other side of the world and so I was there on my own. Even going into the huge dining hall, with all the different food stations, was novel. I had been given my kit and, while proud to be representing my country, I was not enamoured with the ill-fitting, baggy tracksuit that dwarfed me. It's fair to say that I was not expecting much.

I had first met Kelly when I was fifteen; I had gone for some warm weather training in Torremolinos. As time went on the media would try to whip up a rivalry between us, but we were just very different people. She was happy to give her opinions whereas I avoided conflict and didn't like confrontation. That made it hard when she came back to the athletes' village one night after talking to the media.

'Guess what,' she said, 'it's so funny. I've just called you Tadpole to the press.'

'Hilarious,' I said.

I knew it wasn't malicious, but I also knew there was a slight edge to it. She knew the name would stick and it's not the most flattering. I like my psychology and knew there was some meaning to it, because yes, I was tiny and yes, I did worry about whether I could take on the best in the world. I worried about whether I was too small for the event and that no amount of work would compensate for being five feet five inches and going up against people more than half a foot taller. It was my first taste of that environment and, even though Kelly said she meant 'Tadpole' to be affectionate, I was annoyed.

Maybe it fired me up because I started well in Australia. The high jump was particularly good. Kelly managed 1.85 metres but I jumped 1.91, which would have been good enough to win the gold medal in the individual event. I felt like I was flying. I scored four personal bests and was in the shake-up for the silver medal until I was overhauled by Australia's Kylie Wheeler in the 800 metres.

Nevertheless, Kelly was consistent enough to get the gold medal with 6396 points. Wheeler was second and I completed the podium. Afterwards Kelly spoke of 'the little English girl' snapping at her heels. 'She bit me quite hard,' she added. A journalist pointed out that the not-so-subtle Tadpole barb mirrored the way Denise Lewis, the 2000 Olympic champion, had coined her own nick-name for Kelly when she was the rising star. That was news to me but I told the reporter: 'I'd rather be a Princess than a Tadpole.'

Kelly had a moan about her javelin and said she would not be getting major medals unless she improved. 'It was harder here because I had another English girl on my heels,' she said. 'But I wouldn't want it any other way. It made me work harder and I couldn't let her beat me.'

I didn't care. I knew we were just very different personalities. It must be weird when you have been dominating
your event and then someone else comes along. That is
always going to ruffle your feathers, although everyone
knows that a younger athlete will end up being better
than you. I learnt from that. I realized that you are never
going to be at the top forever, so you had better enjoy
your time and be gracious about it. Kelly might have
meant nothing by her remark, but I would never say
anything like that about Katarina Johnson-Thompson,
who is next in line and on the way up now. Kelly had
the gold, but I felt like I had my own. I had added well
over 300 points to my personal best. I went home and
went out into town with Andy. We headed to a bar called
Vodka Revolution and I was the guest at a surprise party,
with friends, family and 'Well done' banners. My friend
Katie's mum had even made me a cake with a medal iced
on it. It was a start. The World Championships were
coming up and now I wanted to have my cake and eat
it.

4

THE ODD
COUPLE

It's almost hard to remember a time before Chell. We clash with as well as complement each other and have a working, dysfunctional relationship. He mocks me and I take the mickey. In some ways we are like an old, married couple, bound together by history and an affection that neither of us ever voices.

It has been a twisting path. The athlete-coach relationship is an odd one in athletics as people often stay together for long periods. I had first met Chell in 1998 when I had just started athletics, and teaming up with him in 1999 was the start of a long, at times turbulent, but successful relationship.

The strange thing for Chell is that he started coaching me when I was a thirteen-year-old schoolgirl. Sometimes he forgets what has happened since, that I have been to university, left home and become a woman. I am still that little girl he used to drive hard. Sometimes that was hard for me because I was a normal girl and I wanted to do lots of things. Chell was a coach and he could see the potential, but it was difficult when I would come home from training in tears about something he'd said. It was not easy for my parents to sit back, especially when my future as an athlete was hanging by a thread, and there were plenty of days when I didn't want to go training.

Chell's job was to push me to the limit and, as time went on, I realized that. I called him the king of cheese and, much later, the DJ Chris Moyles would dub him Minicheddars as a play on his surname – it's quite ironic as they are dead ringers for each other. The cheesy references reflect his insistence on making cheesy statements – nobody can mix a metaphor or do psychobabble quite like him. Once he told me that I should not worry about competing at London because of cockroaches.

'Cockroaches?' I said.

'There was a study,' he began. 'They timed a cockroach running across a strip. Then they timed it with two cockroaches watching. Then they did it with a load watching. They found that even a cockroach runs faster if other cockroaches are watching it.'

'So the moral of the story is . . .'

'You don't have to worry about eighty thousand people in the Olympic Stadium.'

'I wasn't.'

He says there are seven boxes in the brain and, when they are full, that is when rational thought goes out of the window. He tells me to de-clutter my mind and empty the boxes. We rage at each other and there are plenty of times when I storm out of sessions. I get a bit tearful but I never go home. I can't because I know I need to train. I just can't leave. It's always petty things, but he can be patronizing and still speak to me as if I am at junior school.

I stumble out of the house each morning at about 9 a.m. I am not an early riser. I am actually a lazy person in many ways. Then I see Chell and we restart our volatile relationship of little feuds. He will say something sarcastic and I will bite.

Much later we went to see a psychologist. Even though I was a psychology student, I have never been a great advocate of sports psychology. My belief is that it comes from within and that much of what is often said is the blindingly obvious. No matter how much visualizing or role-playing you do, the fact is you also need to work and work, on the track and in the gym and up your own Heartbreak Hill.

Nevertheless, there was a time when we sought help. And, typically for our relationship, it was about how we work together rather than setting any specific sporting goals. Chell says there are four colours of motivation. Red is for drive, green for planning, yellow for innovation and blue for relationships.

The way he put it to me was this: 'If we had to climb a mountain the reds would be saying. "Let's get to the top." The greens would want a map, the yellows would ask if there was another way of getting up and the blues would ask if everybody was happy. I'm very red-yellow and you're red for drive and green for needing a plan.'

He reads a lot and likes his theories so that was interesting. He loves the film *Any Given Sunday* and is prone to making the Al Pacino speech near the end. 'You'll find out life is just a game of inches,' Chell will growl as Pacino.

Ten days before a competition, the tension will rise and we will argue. He will get out his book of stats and tell me what I should be doing. He has a 95 per cent column and a 98. Each one is a percentage of my personal best in each discipline. Tot them up and you get a heptathlon score. He told me: 'On a bad day, with a howling gale and the rain coming down, you should be between those parameters.' People do it in different ways and I do it more by feel and instinct, although I know my scores and what I should be achieving. Then there's my dad, who just watches me for fun and has no idea of any personal bests. He just wants me to do well.

After getting the bronze medal in the Commonwealth Games in Melbourne in March 2006, I rang my mum straightaway. Then I rang Chell. I could tell that he was excited, but I would come to find that there are different ways of dealing with success. I fly on a massive high, but

Chell takes the opposite route. When things go well he actually suffers a bit of a downer. There is also an embarrassed half-hug and handshake afterwards. We are very different people. I will be basking in the moment but he is already looking to the next thing. That is good in some ways, but it's also sad and you can't move too quickly.

I had gone to the European Championships in Gothenburg in early August 2006 and put in another good performance. More personal bests in the shot put and 200 metres put me in a great position, but the competition was fierce and even an improved score of 6287 points was good enough for only eighth. Carolina Klüft won again, maintaining a winning streak that would last for twenty-two competitions and stem back four years to 2002. She was peerless, an incredible champion who looked impossible to beat.

Being up against Klüft and co meant that Gothenburg felt surreal for me, and the following year the World Championships in Osaka, in August 2007, were even more so. In athletics the whole year is based around one major championship – the Europeans, Worlds and, ultimately, the Olympic Games. You might warm up with the indoor season and, while that is serious stuff, it is very much the appetizer for the summer.

Things were changing for me both professionally and personally. Hannah, my friend who also trained with Chell, had stopped doing athletics and was focused on becoming a dentist. She had decided that was a more viable career path for her. I ended up being the only constant, everybody else dropping out, one by one, as time passed, although new people would join to bolster the numbers. We started training next door at the new English Institute of Sport, EIS for short, and in 2006 I also moved with Andy to a little rented terrace house. He was working as a construction site manager and I liked the fact we had something else to talk about at night. I got my degree, a 2:2, which I was happy enough with given that I had missed so much term time.

Any thoughts of an alternative career were on hold for me. I was now immersed in the senior British team and eagerly anticipating the World Championships in Osaka, a sprawling industrial city in Japan. Before that, in early March 2007, I went to the European Indoor Championships in Birmingham. Inevitably, Klüft won, with Kelly second in a new British pentathlon record, just 17 points adrift. I was sixth and frustrated. I watched Nicola Sanders, who would become a friend and room-mate on trips, win the 400 metres, and I looked around the National Indoor Arena. 'Why can't it be me?' I said to myself. 'It's not fair.'

My great-grandad was ninety-four and was really ill at the time, too. I left early because I needed to get home to say goodbye to him, but sadly he died before I made it. He was surrounded by family at home and had lived a full and happy life, but it was terribly sad and made worse by the fact I hadn't been there. Mum was really close to him and was badly affected by his death, but we had lots of good memories. He had a warm, dry sense of humour, as shown by the first time Andy met him. 'Hi, I'm the Godfather,' he said.

It was a difficult time for us all, and Mum in particular, but I was soon back training. I wanted to make up for Birmingham in Osaka in August, but I knew how hard it was going to be. I started brightly and clocked a personal best in the hurdles. The high jump was a solid 1.89 metres. The conditions were stifling, an intimidating heat that meant you were dripping with sweat just walking to the track, but there was no excuse for the abject shot put of just 11.93 metres, my worst of the year. In a flash, any medal chance had gone. That was a horrible feeling.

Klüft was way ahead by the time we got to the 800 metres, the final event. She ended up with a mind-boggling tally of 7032 points. It would be the best performance of her amazing career, topped only by Jackie Joyner-Kersee in the all-time list. I was still in a fight with Kelly for the bronze. I needed to beat her by about two seconds to get it. I gave it everything, left every last vestige of effort on the track, but was only 0.19 seconds clear at the end. It meant I missed out on the bronze by forty-one points.

Maybe people expected me to be mortified after the

shot put, but I actually saw Osaka as an achievement. I was up there with the best, had beaten them at the hurdles and 200 metres, and knew I needed to up my game in the weaker events. The other girls were generous too. Kelly was collared by the BBC trackside interviewer, Phil Jones, and said: 'She's the future. Everybody else better watch out.' At the end of the heptathlon the girls all do a lap of honour together. It is the only event where they do that, but it shows that we have been through the same mill. Klüft put her arm round me and said: 'This will be you one day.' I smiled and thought she was a good example of how to behave as a champion. I had first competed against her in 2005 in Arles in France. I was a nobody and she was the queen of her sport, at the peak of her powers, but I remember her making a point of saying hello to me. She was like the matriarch of the event. She is such a warm person and yet she was one of those who would slap her thighs, scowl and exude aggression before competing.

I have never been that way and Chell would berate me for it. 'You've got to be more aggressive in the way you attack things,' he said.

Even my dad said: 'You've got to give it more, "ugggghh".'

That's not me, though. I liked watching people like Klüft get themselves psyched up, but I was different. Get like that and I would tense up, so I would quietly slip into my blocks instead. People would tell me I wasn't trying, but I always was. It might have added to the image of me as being someone who could be swatted away, and I heard some of the girls commenting on my size in the early days.

'Look at her, she's so small.'

That definitely fired me up on the inside. I wanted to show them, prove a point and prove myself. Over the years, Chell came to realize I was just as aggressive in my own way, but I was different and so he began to use different language.

When it came to exuding that aggression and confidence, the sprinters were in a different world. They strut their stuff and walk through the athletes' village, looking at the women as if eyeing their prey for when they have finished competing. It sometimes had the air of a cattle market. I think you have to be a certain kind of person to be a sprinter. You need a degree of arrogance, although that has changed in recent years with some of them getting older, having kids and ditching the macho posturing.

The aftermath of the World Championships in Osaka was dominated by Kelly's remarks about Lyudmila Blonska, who had been second to Klüft. Blonska set a new Ukrainian national record on the way to her silver medal. For many her return raised question marks, given that she had spent two years out of the sport on a doping ban and had also had a baby during her absence.

'You still have doubts and ninety-nine per cent of us have doubts about certain athletes,' Kelly told BBC Radio. 'Unfortunately, she's one of them. I hope she's clean. I really do because it would please me and everyone else. We'll find out.'

It did not go through my head until Kelly said it, the idea that I might have been cheated out of a medal at my first World Championships, but she was right that people had suspicions. Not a lot was said but there were raised eyebrows and rolled eyeballs. Everyone felt that she was not right. There was something about her, putting up bigger scores than she had done before her ban. It tainted the competition because there is a nice feeling in the heptathlon of all being in it together. Unfortunately, drug-taking is part of sport and you try to balance your cynicism with your naivety. There are the classic things that are supposedly telltale signs – the braces on the teeth, the pitted skin, the deep voice. The grapevine whispers said that, whatever the IAAF – the governing body – had said about the World Championships being drug-free, Blonska was doing something very wrong.

In Britain I do not think there is much of a problem and we lead the way in testing athletes. The 'whereabouts' system means that you have to say where you will be for an hour a day every day. That can be quite hard to keep track of and, in its early days, there were times when I had to change training sessions and I forgot to update my details. It meant I could easily have had a missed test against my name. Three of those and you get a doping ban. It became much easier when you could update your details online and now I have a testing slot of between 6 and 7 a.m. because I know that I am going to be at home at that time.

That can still be uncomfortable and you may be fast asleep when you get the knock on the door and so you stumble downstairs in your PJs. You get to know the testers because they often cover the same area, but sometimes you may get a random test from an IAAF tester, perhaps a German man you've never met before, and so he comes into your house with his gloves and fridge and blood-testing kit.

Once they came and I had been to the toilet two minutes before they arrived. So when they asked for a urine sample I couldn't give one. We sat on the sofa watching BBC *Breakfast*, while I kept going back to the kitchen to swig more water. It is intensely frustrating because you just want to get on with the rest of your day and training. Now I always make sure I hold it in during the waking hours. It can be very uncomfortable but I know I cannot go to the loo before 7 a.m. because if I can't perform for the testers they will have to stay with me until I can.

It is a complicated process too. The athlete has to do everything so you fill in forms, separate the samples, screw the tops and divide the bottles. Now we have to wear gloves. I asked why and I was told that there is a substance people have used which they keep under their fingernails and then flick into the samples to neutralize the drugs.

For me this is another world and I can't comprehend why anybody would go to such lengths to cheat themselves and their rivals. The vast majority of athletes are first and foremost competing for the love of their sport rather than for great financial reward, though of course these days the potential for earning among top athletes is high, so I suppose some people might feel tempted to ditch their morals in order to get up there. But how you could gain any pleasure from success on those terms is beyond me.

When I started competing on the international scene, Chell would always tell me to keep an eye on my water bottle. It sounded fanciful to me, but he was worried that somebody might spike it with something. I do not think anyone would do that, but once he put the thought in my head I decided it was better to be safe than sorry. So 'water carrier' was quickly added to his list of duties.

But you have to take responsibility too. I was always taught that you can never shift the blame. It is why I don't take many supplements because you don't know, 100 per cent for sure, what is in it. There is an online system now where you can type in the ingredients and it will tell you whether it is prohibited or not, but even so

I am sure there are some innocent people being snared in the system. You hear stories about people eating contaminated meat and, in the build-up to London we got an email, warning us to eat only British beef. I am glad the system is so stringent because there are certainly lots of dodgy cases, but it does not make it easy and I just wish that the same measures were implemented in every country. That is why I get annoyed when people start pointing fingers at our sport. Doping is talked about more in athletics, but I imagine it is in all sports. The bad stories never put me off, though. It's a sport I love.

There was some negative reaction when Christine Ohuruogu came back from a one year ban for missing three tests to win the 400 metres title in Osaka. I saw her case as being totally different to anyone who had failed a test. She had missed three tests, but the 'whereabouts' system is a lot clearer now than when it was first introduced. These days we can even text changes to let the testers know we have altered our plans. A lot of people don't appreciate that athletes have the same chaotic lives as everyone else and can forget things, as Christine did. The process is so strict in Britain that I really can't imagine how anyone could attempt to cheat, even if they were that way inclined.

5

CHINA GIRL

In the middle of nowhere, surrounded by snow-clad mountains and a glittering lake, lies the little Austrian town of Götzis. The population fluctuates around the 10,000 mark but it increases each summer when the Hypo-Meeting takes place there. This is one of the biggest events in the calendar for the multi-eventers, outside of the major championships. The standard of the competition is out of kilter with the village-fete atmosphere, cut-throat competition being played out in front of people sunning themselves on grassy banks and tucking into bratwurst.

On Friday 30 May 2008 the sun came out and I met the British press on the infield. We sat down and chatted. I knew that I was being talked up in the media as a good hope for a gold medal at the Olympics in Beijing later that summer. Did I think my rivals now regarded me as a serious contender? 'I fear other people rather than thinking they're walking round worrying about me,' I replied. 'I find it hard to imagine the Olympics. I don't want to think about getting a medal. Deep down I know it's what I'm going for, but I don't want to get wrapped up in it.'

There were other questions about Kelly and Klüft and Blonska. With Carolina deciding to turn her back on the heptathlon and just do the long jump at the Olympics, the pecking order had changed. Carolina was unbeatable, a quite incredible athlete who managed to tether that status to reality without ever losing her generosity. She was widely held in high regard, both as a rival and a person. It was different with Blonska. She had come back from that two-year drug ban in 2007 and won a silver medal at the World Championships. In athletics, there are always nods, winks and innuendos. Suspicions run rife. Rapid improvements or mysterious absences can lead to Chinese whispers of doubt.

That Blonska had come back and scored so highly after her drug ban had caused concern and scepticism among some of the girls. Kelly was always more outspoken than me and again she went public with her remarks, saying that nobody spoke to Blonska. 'We don't support drug cheats,' she added.

I was philosophical and pragmatic about Blonska. She was competing in Götzis and she would be there at the Olympics, probably as the favourite now there was no Carolina. I had to beat her fair and square, whether she was playing by the same rules or not. It is one of the downsides to professional sport, the fact that some people will do anything to win regardless of their conscience.

I had been 363 points adrift of Blonska in Osaka. It was a huge gulf but I had been working hard with Mick Hill and had improved my javelin by five metres. I had once queued up to get Mick's autograph in Sheffield so it felt odd to have him helping me, and I think he probably looked at me and thought, 'This girl can't throw.' If he did he never said it, though, and his boundless enthusiasm rubbed off.

I was gaining something of a reputation for being sweet and nice, and the press guys on the infield mentioned that Chell had said I could be angry and was even known to swear. 'We have arguments but so does every athlete and coach,' I told them. 'I get frustrated and angry and, yes, I swear. My boyfriend and I have decided we use foul language too much so we're going to curb it. When I get frustrated I usually just cry, though. Sometimes, if I've had a bad session, I go home and cry. Other times I count to ten and try to get myself back together.'

There was also mention of Kelly christening me 'Tadpole'. I ducked the question, but the truth is I was hurt by it and did not like it. Chell always finds it harder to bury his feelings and so he let rip. 'The comment was inappropriate and slightly insulting, but it's part of Kelly's make-up and I think that's a bit sad,' he said. 'That's how she competes, by using things like that. It's potentially gamesmanship.'

I wasn't worried about that. I was already aware that the press was trying to build up a rivalry between the two of us. Sometimes this would get amusing, not least when I would read stories about the tadpole developing into a big fish. I am not a zoological expert, but even I knew tadpoles actually became frogs.

But, sitting there on the grass, with Kelly absent through injury and the sun warming my neck, I felt relaxed and ready. I had added three strides to my javelin run-up since Osaka and was increasingly confident. I had had a slight niggle in my right foot but thought it was just down to the bulk of training and none of us were worried about it. I soon realized that it is dangerous to get ahead of yourself in this sport. You live in the moment. It is the only way to get the best out of your performance and the only way to stop fretting about how fate might kick you in the teeth at the cruellest moments.

We had decided not to do much of an indoor season. The focus was all on the summer and China. In Olympic year the hype is cranked up until it is easy to forget that it is just another competition, the same rivals and the same track. The 2008 Hypo-Meeting at Götzis would tell me a lot about where I was and whether I was ready.

I felt good. I had worked like a slave during the winter. It had started at the back end of 2007 with the dreaded hill runs. We go through to Christmas, trekking up and down the big, gradual hill in Chelsea Park in Nether Edge. It was around 150 metres long and we would run up and walk back down for our recovery. If we were walking down too slowly then Chell would bark at us from the bottom and let us know.

'Pick it up! Too slow! Faster!'

The boys might go on ahead, but we were all co-sufferers, caked in mud, breath steaming the freezing air, new aches and pains emerging with each run. We did three sets of five runs up that horrible hill. Then we would do two sets of four on the shorter one. A lot of athletes go warm-weather training in the winter, but I never saw the need. I figured that braving the elements of South Yorkshire was more likely to get me battle-hardened for Beijing.

We would shiver in the car as we were driven back to the EIS for a cup of hot chocolate and then a weights session in the gym. That was our Sunday. I would look at the people getting up late and buying the papers for a long, leisurely read and get jealous.

The sessions inside the EIS were just as bad. The lactic acid filled the muscles and made my legs feel leaden. It was not just my legs either. The acid got into my arms, my bum, my hamstrings. It spread like a black stain until it was constant and then I would feel this crushing pain behind my eyes.

'I've got lactic in my brain,' I told Chell. He shook his head and walked past me as I died quietly on the floor.

As usual I had felt the lactic build up gradually during the session until the one rep where I crossed that line and it flooded through me. In those circumstances there is nothing you can do. You can't feel your legs or your arms. A few of the girls in the group threw up. That happened every session. Their bodies had conditioned them to be sick when they felt the lactic. I hate being sick and never got to that point, so I held it in and came apart instead.

'It's meant to be hard,' Chell would say to us. 'This is the worst it can ever get.'

He reminded me of that in Götzis. 'You've done the work,' he told me. 'It will be painful but not as bad as that.' As it turned out, he was wrong.

That night we went to the athletes' parade in the town. Derry Suter, my soft tissue therapist, came with me. There was a barbecue and the heptathletes all had to run down a path between the crowds, hi-fiving all the kids as we went. The next step of the time-honoured programme that never changes took place in the town hall. Each athlete was called up onto the stage. This was my first time in Götzis but I would come to find that the presenter would say the same thing to me year after year.

'I'm small, too,' she would begin, 'but *I've* got my heels on.'

I smiled and accepted the rose that they gave to each athlete. It was the ancient side of old-fashioned, but not as bad as the time they used to hold a Miss Heptathlete type of beauty pageant before the competition in Desenzano del Garda in Italy. Quite how they got us all to do that I don't know, but we would parade around the stage there before the judges voted on who was worthiest of this high honour. I won it once but I do not count it among my greatest achievements.

The trappings of Götzis disguised how important it was, and on Saturday 31 May we all turned up for the start of competition. There was little chat among the competitors. I am quite friendly with Jessica Zelinka, from Canada, and would talk to Hyleas Fountain, the best American, but there is nobody I would call a close friend. I compartmentalize my life and have friends and rivals, business colleagues and family.

The competition began, as ever, with the 100 metres hurdles, my favourite event, and I did not feel right from the start. For me it was a rubbish time and the vague niggle I had had beforehand was still there. It is easy to panic as an athlete, viewing every little ache or pain into impending doom, but I said to myself, 'What's going on?' Then it got really bad in the high jump.

The sense of panic was rising now. At first my fear

was that I would not be able to get another jump in and I needed the points. Then it grew into a fear of having to pull out of the event and I did not want to do that because I had finished every heptathlon that I had started. It would be some time before these doubts and fears would merge into the deep, dark realization that the entire Olympic dream was in the balance.

Neil Black, the UK Athletics physio and future performance director, gave me some treatment at the side of the track.

'It feels like the ankle's blocked,' I said. 'Like it needs cracking or pulling or something.'

Neil manipulated it and it felt looser. I tried a run and stopped quickly.

'I can't,' I said. The panic was now all-engulfing.

Still, I went to the shot put and set a personal best. That event allows you to get onto your toes and so it was a different part of the foot I was using. But a PB? Clearly, it did not seem to be anything too serious. And then came the final event of that first day, the 200 metres. I clocked 23.59 seconds. That was a poor time, and in the home straight I felt as though I was going backwards. I struggled to push off my right foot at all, and by the end I was second overall, behind Anna Bogdanova, and I could hardly walk.

I struggled across the infield with Neil to get my stuff.

'Walk as naturally as you can,' he said.

'Okay,' I replied, but every step hurt. 'It's really sore.'

I went into the physio room under the grey stand and my ankle was encased in ice. Not for one minute did I think the Olympics were in doubt, but I was gutted. I could see training schedules and plans being thrown up in the air. I could see sessions being lost and, for someone who thrives on a plan, it was an awful prospect.

Chell was being upbeat and said: 'It'll be fine, it'll be fine.'

The press guys came in and did an interview. That was the hardest thing. I just wanted to cry my eyes out, but I didn't want to be secretive. I was given an old pair of bright yellow crutches that someone had found at the back of the stand and went back to the hotel.

I put on a brave face. I was sure it was nothing, I said. Chell said it was just a precaution. Dave Collins, the UK Athletics performance director said he hoped people would not go all Chicken Licken and suggest the sky was falling down. He had reason to be concerned, with Paula Radcliffe still on crutches too after being diagnosed with a stress fracture to the femur just two weeks before.

That night, back at the hotel, it began to sink in how serious this might be and I was distraught. I'd never pulled out of a heptathlon and I was anxious, not knowing what was wrong. I went to my hotel room and cried. My grandparents were over that weekend. There had been a story in one of the papers saying how, when I was young and wavering, my grandad gave me a pound for every personal best. I spoke to him and he said: 'A pound! It was a fiver. Everyone in the village thinks I'm tight.' I said, 'All right, Grandad, I've got other things to worry about.'

Neil sorted me a flight and I flew back early on Sunday. I rang Andy, who was awaiting my call and drove down. I was in floods of tears when I saw him because my mindset had darkened.

'I'm not going to the Olympics, I'm not going to the Olympics.'

I took a call from Chell who tried to lift my spirits.

'I'm not going to the Olympics, am I?'

'Yes, of course you are, everything's fine.'

Neil had told me to get ice on it and try to do some rotating exercises before he picked me up and drove me back to the hospital the next day. I think the potential outcomes were getting more depressing with each person who told me that there was nothing to worry about.

The MRI scan took forty minutes and the CT one took five. I hobbled from the hospital to the Olympic Medical Institute to see Paul Dijkstra, the UK Athletics doctor, who explained that if there was a lot of white on the scan then that showed the inflamed area. When we looked at the scans it was like snow. There was a lot of white.

'You have a stress fracture in your navicular and a

stress fracture in your metatarsal,' he said. In total I actually had three fractures. I couldn't believe it.

'How bad are they?'

His look told me everything and Doc, being a clinician, was not one to sugar-coat the truth. 'You're not going to the Olympics,' he said. It blew me away. All my family had been telling me it would be OK and, deep down, I'd been convincing myself of the same. Neil gave me a hug and had to leave to get me some tissues, but there was more to come. 'It's a serious injury,' Doc said. Then he told me my career might be over. I was twenty-two years old and potentially finished. I cried some more.

I went back to my cell-like room and felt like a condemned woman. I rang my parents and Chell. I could tell from his voice that he was really upset. Derry Suter later told me just how bad Chell had been and that he was really cut up.

I had to stay down in London because I needed a bone density scan. That was horrible because the OMI rooms are like student accommodation. I sat in my room and mulled it over. Neil took me out to a restaurant that night. It was a blur. I don't know how he coped. I was crying all the time and my face was puffy and red. I don't know what the waiter must have thought.

Beforehand, Doc had said that if it was just a stress fracture of the metatarsal then it would not be that bad and we could try to make the Olympics. It turned out to be worse, affecting that back part of the foot behind the metatarsals where the blood supply is so poor.

I didn't want to make it worse and break it. We could have tried to speed up the process by staying off my feet for three weeks, instead of eight, and then having an operation to put screws in to hold it. It was a massive gamble but I was not tempted at all. I desperately wanted to go to Beijing, but not at the risk of ending my career.

The response was incredible. I was so glad to get home to Sheffield and my family and Andy. I had texts, e-mails and cards from all manner of people. Paula Radcliffe passed on her number and said she was there if I needed to talk. I thought that was an impressive thing to do. Paula has been through so many injury crises, but the fact she could be bothered to offer to help when she, too, was racing against time and an ailing body to be fit for the Olympics was quite something.

Another person who rang up was Nathan Douglas, the triple jumper, who had missed the World Championships the previous year with a hamstring injury. Everyone said, 'Keep your chin up', but when it is actually happening you don't want to listen. It feels like your world is falling apart. Words can't restore that. Nathan understood that. He said people told him he would be back but all he could think about was the missed opportunity. Sometimes it is best not to mollycoddle people. The truth hurts, but half-truths are worse.

Above left: Proud new mum Alison with baby Jess.

Above right: Daddy's girl.

Right: My Spice Girls moves.

Below: Me and little sister Carmel in Grandma and Grandad's garden.

Teenage kicks – doing the hurdles at Don Valley in 2000.

All those bribes pay off – with Grandad and my bronze medal.

'All I want to do is stand on the top of the medal podium.' With Jennifer Oeser (silver) and Kamila Chudzik (bronze).

JessicaEnnis.net

Above: Grinning and bearing it – my foot is encased in my rehab boot during the lay-off in 2008.

Left. Sheffield steel – sparks fly at the Forgemasters shoot in 2009.

Below: After winning my world title a big hug from Andy was awaiting me.

Left: Myla – my favourite distraction.

The girls – Katie, Georgina, Lauren and Charlotte (bottom) and Lorna (inset) – help celebrate my 2009 world title back in Sheffield.

Stepping out – at the *Cosmopolitan* awards in 2010.

The raining champ – I return to Götzis for the first time since the injury in 2010.

Hard at work at the Team GB training camp in Portugal before the European Championships in 2010.

Going round the bend – and winning the 200m at the European Championships in Barcelona.

Above: Even Chell enjoyed himself in Barcelona.

Right: The cursed long jump – this time in Götzis.

Below: The new European champion celebrates.

Mick Hill can't resist a good demo.

The glamour of competition – having an ice bath after Götzis watched by Chell (left), Bricey (centre) and Derry (right).

Above: Losing my grip – the world title disappears on the slippery javelin runway at the World Championships in South Korea in 2011.

Inset: 'How bad is it?' Chell delivers the truth.

Left: That sinking feeling – Chernova celebrates after winning my world title in 2011.

Above: Trying to be happy with my silver medal.

Kelly sent me a couple of supportive messages. I thought she had a good chance to take the gold now if she was fit, with Blonska and Tatyana Chernova also in the mix. I didn't think anyone had looked outstanding on that first day in Götzis, so it was quite open, but that just made it worse, to have to sit at home and try not to think, 'That could have been me.' I still don't know to this day who won that year in Götzis.

It got to me. There was a *Sky News* report on my injury when I left the hospital on crutches. My dad says he remembers flicking on the TV, seeing that and thinking, 'Poor kid.' He also saw the tears. 'Seeing you cry in public was hard,' he said. 'That's not Jess. You just don't do that.'

There were so many flowers in the house that it looked like a funeral parlour. It was hard not to wallow in self pity or become consumed by a flood of what-ifs and why-mes? I knew that everyone got injuries, that they were part and parcel of an athlete's life, but to devote your life to something and have it snatched away was a bit like suffering a bereavement. You've lost something that is part of you. It's devastating. Heartbreaking.

It was only later that I wondered what it was like for my parents and for Chell. It can't have been easy for any of them. My dream is the same as Chell's so he was suffering too. But you get consumed by what is happening to you alone. Later, my mum gave an interview where she explained what it was like for her. She said: 'It was horrible, just horrible, not being able to put something right for your child. She was absolutely heartbroken. She was living in a little terrace and we went round with a card and some flowers. She had this big contraption that she had to put her foot in twice a day – I've still got no idea what it was. She was desperately down, saying, "My career's over", "What's the point?" I think it helped that her boyfriend, Andy, had broken his leg really badly playing football and she had seen him go through that. She had supported him but, of course, it was *her* career.'

I had looked after Andy after he'd had his accident and in some ways his was even worse. He had broken his tibia and fibula playing football and it had taken nine months to heal properly. It was horrible for him and he did moan – can you get this for me, can you do that? – but now the roles were reversed. I had not coped that well with Andy's injury when I had gone to the hospital and seen him with an external fixator, effectively a cage, attached to his leg, holding it together. The nurse showed me how to clean the pins. She explained that when he bent his leg the flesh would tear. The thought of that, combined with seeing someone I love in pain, plus the claustrophobic heat in there, meant that before I knew it I was coming around on the floor, with a group of faces all peering down on me and an alarm bell sounding.

I heard Andy's voice. 'You've always got to be the centre of attention, haven't you?' he was saying with a smile on his face.

This time I was. Mum set up a rota of family and friends so there was always someone with me. I think her background in working with people facing crises helped. She knew loneliness can be debilitating for those feeling low and Andy still had a job to go to. Carmel was also on the rota. By now we got on great and the teenage sparring days seemed a long way off. I think a lot of siblings are probably like that and only really become good friends when they are separated. Now she's also got a career of her own, working with nursery school kids and showing her caring side off to great effect.

I was told I'd be on crutches for two months. Up until then I had been lucky with injuries. There was the time as a kid when I had fallen off a roundabout and gashed my head open. Then there was the Pippi Longstocking day. But in terms of my athletic career, I had been lucky. And now my luck had turned.

There were some very dark days after that. Dave Collins asked me if I wanted to go to the Olympics anyway to taste the whole experience. It would be good for London in another four years, but that seemed an age away. It was impossible to think about 2012 when I was flat on my back for an hour a day on a magnetic bed. It had been shipped in from UK Athletics and had a hood that went over the leg that looked like a Dalek's head and it weighed about a ton. We had to break it down to get it up the stairs. Andy said that it used up so much electricity that when I switched it on the entire street went dark.

I had two 20-minute sessions on an Exogen machine, too, designed to heal bones via ultrasound waves. It was not proven that it helped but I was prepared to try anything. My attitude was 'why not?' If I was ever seriously ill then I am the sort of person who would go from faith healer to acupuncturist in search of a cure. Someone posted a message on my website saying, 'It's not how far you fall but how high you bounce.' It was all nice and encouraging but the words and messages were papering over the cracks in my life and fractures in my foot.

I could see myself literally fading away. As an athlete you work so hard to build yourself up, but I could see my leg getting thinner and thinner. I was forced to watch myself go backwards while the talk in all the papers and on the TV was about those athletes who were in the shape of their lives and were going to go for medals in Beijing.

There was also the issue of money. I felt terrible because I knew how much my family had spent booking tickets and hotels for Beijing. The cost was around £6,000 and I felt guilty that they had lost that. 'It's only money, isn't it?' my mum said, but I knew they didn't have a lot.

We never have had. I had always been taught the value of money and it was an added burden to think my family had lost so much because of me.

There was the boredom as well as the depression. I went on the Internet and got even more down via Google search. I read for hours and found lots of examples of people who had suffered with the same sort of injuries for their entire careers. It is definitely not healthy to use the Internet to diagnose yourself; it is certainly unlikely to cheer you up.

I had a protective boot put on the foot. Bill Ribbans, a top orthopaedic surgeon, handled the process. He was caring and brilliant and got the time frame right – two long, hard, bitter months. My physio Ali worked with him to create a rehab programme, and there was a lot of travelling to and from Northampton to see him, and then to and from London for more scans. I spent ages sitting in the car and simmering in near silence, angry that this should happen to me.

The year was a write-off so I looked ahead to 2009 and the indoor season the following spring. Then, looming far enough in the distance to be a realistic goal but not too far away to feel intangible, were the World Championships in Berlin in August 2009. I went to the gym and did weights and core exercises, although they were literally exercises in frustration as I could not put any weight on my foot.

Ali and Derry were devastated too. They felt they were in some way to blame, because it was their area of expertise, but never for one moment did I think like that. The unfortunate thing is that with a stress fracture you hammer away in training and it's only when the bones fracture – literally when the cracks appear, if you like – that you feel pain and know anything is wrong. They wished they could have done something but they did everything right. It's such a vague feeling around the navicular that it is hard to diagnose anything unless you have scans every day. I told them they were not to blame at all, because I knew that we were a team and that Chell, Ali, Derry, Mick and I were all collectively heartbroken.

They responded with a huge show of faith. Ali had been working with UK Athletics for a long time, nursing Kelly Holmes through her chronic injuries to a double gold in Athens in 2004, and I sensed she was trying to phase out of it all. I was not sure of Derry's plans either, but Olympics are turning points for lots of people, not just athletes, and many choose to do other things after them. They sat me down during those rehab days and Derry said: 'Ali and I have had a chat and we've decided we're going through until 2012 with you.' I broke out into a rare smile because it felt like such a commitment from them. 'All of us are going for it,' he added. 'We've got unfinished business.'

Ali had already helped a lot, not only with her

expertise but also with her attitude. She said she thought things happened for a reason. I believe that too. I am not religious but I am fatalistic. I believe you have a journey in life but I don't believe that it's all out of your control. I also think you have to be able to blame external things sometimes. If you constantly blame everything on the internal then it's very hard to get over a disappointment. I don't mean you always want to be able to say that it was the fault of the weather or the track that you didn't perform at your best, and I am not advocating passing the buck. But it helps if you can look outside yourself.

Not that I felt that in those early days. I was so down and needed to get my head around it, but before long I wanted to do the rehab. I wanted to get down to the EIS, but I was up and down. Some days I felt like that, flushed with a new sense of positivity and wanting to do the pool sessions or the programme I had for my upper body, but on others I felt terrible and angry that everybody else was getting on with their careers.

I tried another way of coping one night. My friends dragged me out for a night on the town. I didn't want to go because I was on crutches and wallowing in misery, but I went and enjoyed myself. A bit too much as it turned out. It was the drunkest I have ever been in my life. I got home and could not get the key in the door. Andy was asleep because he had to go to work the next day, so I struggled along in my drunken state and eventually went around the back. Andy later told me that he found me sprawled out on the back step, crutches and rehab boot all over the place. It was probably not that professional but I needed the therapy. For one night only, I just had to get hammered.

Andy had to drive me everywhere. I'd lie across the back seat with my leg up, helpless. I hated the inactivity and the dependency. I didn't like going out, though, because my hands hurt from the crutches so, more often than not, I would stay at home, watching the box set of *Smallville* that Andy had bought me, detailing the early, pre-Superman life of Clark Kent. Maybe the following year I could make a similar leap from ordinary Sheffield girl to something quite different. Ultimately, I came to accept that you can't undo the past.

I was touched by people's kindness and I knew I was far from unique. I strove to keep perspective and told myself that things happen for a reason, even if you have no idea what that reason may be. I said that maybe I would look back in four years from an Olympic podium and be glad that this happened. I might not have believed it, but I went back to my *Smallville* life, working away while the rest of the world congregated in Beijing, and told myself this was not meant to be my time.

I did watch the Olympics on television. It was hard for Kelly because just three months earlier she had been in hospital with kidney failure and she had not done a heptathlon for twelve months. She still ran two personal bests and got a season's best in another event on the first day, but unfortunately she didn't make the podium. Nataliya Dobrynska was crowned champion with 6733 points, Blonska was second, completing a Ukrainian one-two, and America's Hyleas Fountain took the bronze medal.

Days later the suspicions gave way to reality and it emerged that Blonska had failed a drug test. I cannot say I was surprised. It was not just that she had previously been banned, it was the fact she had come back from her ban and had turned into a sort of Superwoman, scoring far more points than she had previously. The timeline of cheats in track and field meant that this scenario could not go unchallenged.

When she was stripped of the medal and banned, I inevitably began to think back to the World Championships when I had finished fourth. I had admonished myself for not doing better in the shot put, and so to find I had been beaten by someone who had twice failed a drug test made me angry. That's the real pain of doping: the impact it has on the innocent.

Kelly later said that she had actually seen Blonska take something while competing in Beijing. It happened as they walked out of the call room. Blonska's husband, who is also her coach, handed her something. Kelly said she followed her to the long-jump pit and saw that she had a phial. Who knows what was in there? Maybe it was something to mask the drugs. Maybe it was innocent. But Kelly stared her in the eye, daring her to take the substance, and she did just that.

I found the whole thing depressing. The heptathlon is such a tough event that there is a sense of unity among the athletes. You are in it for yourself, of course, but you are also in it together, straining every sinew and driving your body and mind to breaking point in pursuit of the same thing. In women's athletics, it's the ultimate test in many ways. To then find someone has ruined all that was hard to take.

After my one night out, I worked hard that winter. It was some of the hardest work I have done because not being able to run is horrible for me. It's what I do, what I like. It gives me a sense of purpose. I toiled away in the gym and on the cross-trainer. Then I went down for my last scan.

My dad came with me. He is such a placid, kind person. I think he may have sensed me drifting back in time so he would try to cheer me up. 'You know what, Jess, there is one good thing about not having to go to Beijing.'

'Oh yeah, what's that?'

'No smog. Tell you the truth, I'd been really worried about my asthma.'

The scan was clear. I came out smiling and my dad

gave me a hug. He drove me back up the M1 to Sheffield, but stopped at Watford Gap services on the way.

'Let's have burgers to celebrate,' he said. I smiled again.

6

OPEN WHEN CHAMPION

Trying to get to the top of the podium was a personal dream, but there were lots of people working away behind the scenes to make it happen. In a way it was like a house of cards, with me at the top and a broad base shouldering the load, and like a house of cards I knew it could all come crashing down at any time.

It was during my time injured that my team became complete. I had an agent but was looking for someone new and Chell got introduced to Jane Cowmeadow. When we met we clicked and have never looked back. A lot of agents will get you to do anything as long as they get their cut, but Jane only wanted me to do things that were right for me. And, to be honest, in 2009 the opportunities were still pretty scarce for a broken athlete hobbling around with a fractured foot and a broken dream. Jane's arrival was a key moment, though, and completed the network of support specialists that people would refer to as Team Ennis. This is the team sheet in full.

TONI MINICHIELLO (Coach): Ah, Chell, what can I say about him? We had been together for more than a decade and sometimes he still treated me like that thirteen-year-old schoolgirl. He was getting better, though, and the main thing was he was a very good coach who devised top programmes. Yes, he would drive me to distraction at times with his criticism and cheese, but I also knew he got the best performances out of me.

ALISON ROSE (Physiotherapist): Ali is such a lovely person and she is passionate about what she does. She had been at the top for a long time, but she did not rest on her laurels and was always looking for ways to further her knowledge. She was also prepared to go the extra mile for me. Many physios work 9 to 5, but Ali would make the effort to see me on a Saturday if that was what was needed. During the injury she rang me every day, asking how it was feeling. Another string to her bow was her capacity to listen. If I had had an argument with Chell then I would go to see her and she let me whinge away. It was somewhere I found I could go to clear my head. She might have a quiet word with Chell afterwards. 'Say this to her,' she might suggest, planting seeds to make it all better. There was never any reason for her to feel bad about what had happened – it was just one of those horrible things sport threw at us.

She put me on the rehab programme and I saw her once a week for a general check-up. I might have felt fine, but she would tell me things were out of line. Ribs could move out of place and the liver and kidneys could get stuck and impact on nerves. She taught me so much.

DERRY SUTER (Soft-tissue therapist): I saw Derry twice a week. He is a caring chatterbox who works a painful brand of magic. Ali corrected my skeletal frame and Derry did the hard work of releasing my muscles. He's brilliant, but brutal, scraping his elbow along my spine, digging his fingers into the soles of my feet. When I was doing my rehab I felt Ali and Derry really believed in me and that was a huge help during the dark days.

MICK HILL (Javelin coach): All the years of competition had taken their toll and he had needed a lot of operations, but Mick would ignore the shoulders, knees and hips, put on his boots, roll back the years and throw with me.

His passion and enthusiasm were just what I needed because the javelin was not an event that came naturally for me. So we used a contraption with a weight attached to a pulley with a javelin handle on the other end. I was not the biggest of throwers, so he worked on technique, using my whole body to get the sequence right.

It took me a long time before I could afford a javelin of my own. Now I keep them in the shed. You choose them according to length of throw. I throw pink ones (fifty-metre ones). That means they will fly and turn over at the right time. If I threw a seventy-metre javelin it would never turn and you need the tip to hit the ground first. Mick will look around, test the wind, smile at the grey sky and say: 'Great day for throwing.' To him, it's always a great day.

PAUL BRICE (Biomechanist): Some of this went over my head, but Bricey would monitor performance on a laptop, draw up charts and then write reports. He was the numbers man. When we were trying to sort out the long jump, he would tell me that it was pointless to tear down the runway at ten metres per second if I slowed to seven metres just before take-off. He was looking for greater consistency and performance and he did that by breaking it all down, piece by piece. Although he is a great man who spent a lot of time getting me to where I needed to be, his banter left a lot to be desired.

PETE LINDSAY (Psychologist): The most work I have done with him is working through the respective psychologies of Chell and me and how we can best communicate in pressured situations. When something goes wrong I need instant feedback. Chell prefers to go away, think about it and then come back with a plan. To me that seemed that he did not care, but it was just different ways of working. Pete also worked with me on dealing with the pressure of the competitions and coping with the lows and frustrations brought on by injury.

STEVE INGHAM (Physiologist): Steve was always on hand to give advice on preparing for the dreaded 800 metres, from the types of sessions I need to do in preparation for it, to what I need to do to ensure I get through a race, with all that it might throw at me physically. He was so knowledgeable, and I really felt that if anyone could make doing an 800 metres bearable, he was the man.

JANE COWMEADOW (Agent): Jane, and her right-hand woman, Suzi Stedman, became good friends after we teamed up in 2009. Jane was more like a second mum, not just cutting deals but making sure my family were in the right place in stadiums and doing things that would bring her no return. She was always going that extra mile to make life as easy as possible so that I could give training and competing my total focus.

That was Team Ennis, all cogs in a machine to keep things rolling. Every member of the team played a big part in reviving me during that bitter post-Beijing winter. Ultimately, it was my life and my career, but you need your help, friends and sounding boards. So when the gloom slowly lifted, I wrote off the year. I scrubbed Beijing from my mind and instead pencilled in the IAAF World Combined Events Challenge in Desenzano del Garda for my heptathlon comeback at the start of May 2009.

It was a deeply unsettling time. Dave Collins was sacked as performance director after the team only managed four medals in Beijing, with Christine getting the only gold. I had been scared of him when I came into the senior ranks, but in truth, it did not make much difference to me who was in charge. One of Dave Collins's innovations was to give athletes marks out of ten for their performance. He did that at the European Championships in Gothenburg and it caused a big fuss. Some people were given two out of ten and even Paula Radcliffe went public and said: 'I absolutely hate it.' I am not sure what he wanted to achieve by it but I can't even remember my score.

His replacement was Charles van Commenee. He had been involved with UK Athletics before as technical director of combined events and Chell had told him that he had a rising star and tried to get him interested in me back in the early days. He had replied I was too young.

He was famed for his 'wimp' comment directed at Kelly and he ruffled some feathers with his approach, but again he did not have much to do with me. I was working with Chell and my team and was left to get on with it.

I was wrapped up in my own struggles anyway. The injury was bad and then Chell dropped his own bombshell as we did a long-jump session.

'Why don't you change your take-off foot?' he said.

I laughed incredulously. 'No way!'

'Just give it a go.'

'No!'

The idea of having to change my take-off foot was simply awful. The long jump was an event I was already struggling with and now, on the comeback trail, with the World Championships looming, he wanted me to reprogramme my brain.

The problem was that I would charge down the runway and stick out my right foot as if it was the high jump. That acted as a brake. It would arc me into the air rather than through it, and that meant I was dropping short. Chell described it as educating the neural pathways to get the left foot to behave differently. 'I want you flying like a plane off the end of an aircraft carrier.'

I was reluctant to change as I thought it would only make things worse. People spend years training to make things instinctive, so to then go back to basics and rebuild it from scratch sounded daunting. Yet, in the back of my mind, I was scared about the injury too. I wanted to jump like I had before, but it was only now that I considered the force that went through the body with every jump. I thought, 'What if I never master this event? If this doesn't go right then I've wrecked everything.' So, reluctantly, we started to rebuild me.

I did little drills to start with but it got harder and harder. Every little niggle, real or imagined, sent me into panic mode. I didn't know if the bone would fuse properly and I knew I might end up with bone spurs, which could cause pain, swelling and worse, leaving me unable to achieve all that I wanted.

Bricey came along and helped. He explained how I

planted my foot with my toe and then collapsed through the knee. I treated it like a high jump, one of my favourite events, and had my foot out in front of me, when it should be underneath. We looked at videos, frame by frame, and tried to correct things and search for the small gains. The injury had given me little choice. I had to protect the broken foot and so I worked slavishly to get used to jumping the other way round.

I made my comeback in January 2009 at the Northern Athletics Senior Indoor Championships. I did the 60 metre hurdles and came second in 7.56 seconds. It was a low-key event and pretty low-grade running, but it was a start and I was not injured. After months in the gym I felt like an athlete again. A weight lifted.

I then went to Cardiff for the McCain Inter City Cup Final and long-jumped 5.98 metres. That was pretty appalling and did not fill me with confidence about the new system. To put it in context, I consider 6.40 metres my minimum requirement in a heptathlon. I was miles off.

We went to a variety of small meetings at the start of that year to ease me back in. I threw the javelin in Cleckheaton, Bedford and Sheffield, topping 40 metres regularly. The shot put has never been one of my best events, but it was okay. However, I don't think I realized quite how much tension I was feeling until I went to Desenzano in May for my first heptathlon since Götzis.

The hurdles was first up. All I think about when I'm in the blocks are the first few strides. Get them right. That's what matters. I thought back to all the drills we had done at the EIS. All those times we set out the hurdles. We used two sets, one silver and one red. That was because the video analysis showed that I lengthened my stride after the sixth hurdle. The colours were a visual aid to remind me to chop my stride and keep the rhythm and speed. I lined up, got away well and felt good. I kept my stride length right. I did not clout any hurdles. That can be costly, in flesh as well as time, as I knew from the time John, a training partner, clipped a hurdle down at the EIS. I went over to him and was laughing because he had taken a calamitous tumble, but then I realized his face was ghostly white. He lifted his shorts and I realized the base of the hurdle had flipped and scythed through his thigh, tearing a strip and leaving the muscle exposed. When Chell saw the damage he had to go over to the other side of the track and lie down with his feet up. I went to get some ice, while John turned whiter. That was the worst-case scenario. This time I did not hit anything. I got it right and flew over the line in a time of 12.98 seconds. That was good. Dip below 13 seconds and it's a solid start in my head.

It went on from there. The high jump was good, 1.90 metres, and I felt no problems with my foot. Inevitably, I thought about what had happened in Götzis, but this time it was fine. I had my ping back. The shot put was okay, 13.19 metres, and it was a good first day, but the following morning I would face the long jump and javelin, the two events that would be highlighted as Achilles heels all the way from Lake Garda to East London.

I did well enough in both. The long jump was 6.16 metres, which was a disappointment but not a disaster. It was a work-in-progress and I was in a good place in the competition. I threw the javelin 42.70 metres and then clocked a career-best 2 minutes 9.88 seconds in the awful 800 metres. It meant I had won convincingly. I was more than 500 points clear of the field and it was quickly pointed out that I was third on the all-time UK list with 6587 points. Immediately, I was installed as one of the favourites for the World Championships, but I also knew how much harder that was going to be.

I even stayed smiling at the post-competition banquet. I heard the announcer say my name a few times, but she was speaking in Italian and so I was not sure what she was talking about. Everyone at my table said they were calling me to go up and get my trophy. I traipsed up to the stage, oblivious to the strange looks I was getting from certain quarters, and stood at the side of the stage. The woman kept talking and slowly it dawned on me that they had not called out my name at all and had merely been discussing the day's events. I had little choice but to stand there for what seemed like an eternity and cringe away in silence. It was one of the most excruciating experiences of my life. There was a lot of sniggering and, when I finally made it back to my table, flushed with embarrassment, Ali was creased up with laughter. 'I thought you were my friends,' I said, laughing.

Before a competition the tension is always ratcheted up in those last days. Andy says he can pinpoint my mood swings in terms of miles. When we set off in the car to a competition I am fine and chatty, but by the time we have got to the other side of Snake Pass, the A57 road between Sheffield and Manchester, I am quiet and snappy. Grandad tells me I was the same as a junior, gradually receding more and more into myself the closer I got to an athletics track.

Andy had decided to travel out to Berlin to watch the World Championships. My agent Jane was also there, but my mum and dad had decided to stay at home. We had talked about it beforehand; they knew I felt bad because they had lost so much money on the Beijing trip that never was.

'Will you be offended, Jess, if we don't go?' my mum asked.

'It's up to you,' I replied.

'I just don't want you worrying about anything else. It would be best for you to just concentrate.'

My dad smiled and gave me a hug. 'Make sure you ring us, though.'

I have only recently started to appreciate how hard it is for my parents. My dad says it's awful as a spectator.

'I love watching you do the hurdles because you are so good at it, but I hate it at the same time,' he told me. 'It's where it can all go wrong. One mistake.'

My mum says it's horrible too. She just wants me to do well for myself, but I knew they would be nervous and fretting at home, and that not being there would just let their imaginations think the worst. My mum is not superstitious, but she later told me that, after the injury, she just did not want to jinx anything. Three days before I competed she stopped eating. It was a crippling fear, not about me winning or losing, but about me being happy. For an athlete those two things are intertwined, and happiness was now dependent on the world title bid.

The Olympic Stadium in Berlin is swathed in memories. Figures of famous athletes stand outside and there is a plaque to commemorate Jesse Owens' feats at the 1936 Olympics. He broke down barriers and humiliated Hitler, but that was several generations ago. Although I could feel the echoes of the past, I was in my bubble, in the here and now.

It had been a hell of a journey up to Berlin and it had not been totally smooth behind the scenes. Chell often struggles to bite his lip when he senses injustice and so he gave an interview ahead of the World Championships where he voiced his grievances. 'There was a great team around Jess and it's been decimated,' he said. 'London will be harder now so it's unfortunate that

I've lost a nutritionist, a physiologist and a performance analyst.'

He said it was down to changes at UK Athletics and people moving jobs. Two had moved into other sports and Steve Ingham took over as lead physiologist at the English Institute of Sport so would not be working directly in athletics. 'It's a step into the future via a crystal ball and I don't work on crystal balls,' he said.

For me the biggest worry was that Ali Rose would not be one of the physios travelling with the team to Berlin. After what I had been through with my foot, all the days, weeks and months of rehab, I trusted her implicitly. The fact she would not be in Berlin was a hammer blow. However, in the end we found a way for Ali to come out and I breathed a huge sigh of relief.

Toni was incredulous that Alison had not been considered necessary. 'The person who knows how to fix Jess between events is Alison Rose, so I had to get her there any way I could,' he said in an interview. 'Christ, do you think Manchester United don't cover everything? I am sure a lot of people will draw kudos if she wins, but they say success has many friends but failure is an orphan.'

I knew what he meant. People make a fuss about you when you do well, but you are quickly forgotten about when you are injured or not performing well. It's a fickle world and I prefer people to treat you the same way in the good and bad times.

I led the world rankings going into Berlin in August 2009, but I knew it was going to be tough. There was Nataliya Dobrynska, the Olympic champion from Ukraine. She was far taller and had more muscle than me. Dobrynska trained in a decrepit stadium on the outskirts of Kiev, daubed with graffiti and with holes in the black indoor track. She said she carried a spade in her boot to dig over the long-jump pit and that teenagers gathered in the shadow of the grey stadium wall to drink and make mischief. She was tough.

There was also Tatyana Chernova, a tall, thin Russian who had a habit of doing handstands to warm up and had taken a bronze in Beijing at the age of just twenty. All the best heptathletes in the world were present and the nerves reverberated around my brain and body.

I started well. I shot out of the blocks in the hurdles, crossed the line and looked to the scoreboard. It flashed up 12.93 seconds. I'd run a lifetime best of 12.81 seconds a few weeks earlier, but I was not complaining. I had not started that well in Desenzano and so I was on my way. In the back of my mind a voice was telling me that something was going to go horribly wrong, or that I would fall over, so it was a huge relief to finish safely.

It was hard for all of us to keep our cool in the white heat of competition. There were twenty-nine of us vying for the same prize. The high jump was next and I cleared 1.92 metres. That was above average for me and I felt something good happening. You can never get ahead of yourself in the heptathlon because there are seven traps, but I was building a lead over the rest.

And then it looked as if it might all come crashing down. Dobrynska opened the shot put with a mighty throw of 15.81 metres. I managed only 13.07 and then a disastrous 12.55 metres. It meant that, as I stepped up for my third and last throw, a big lead had been whittled away. Deep down I knew the world title attempt probably rested on this throw. I picked up the shot, took position and tried to clear my mind. De-clutter the boxes. Chell always says the shot put is not about muscle but timing. It's like a golf swing. Too fast or too slow and you will shank or slice it.

I think I was helped by the training we had done with John, the decathlete with the ripped thigh muscle. Often we would put out markers in training and bet each other that we would outdo each other. The stakes would be something like a chocolate bar or negotiating with Chell to get an easier running session. Sometimes I'd strike the wager with Chell himself, and before Berlin I put a cone out to a whopping 14.50 metres.

'If I get that then we're running 400 metres, not 600,' I said.

'You'll get nowhere near it,' he laughed.

But I did. I needed that incentive. Training can be boring. I needed that extra motivation, that adrenaline rush. Maybe that is why I managed to slow it down on that final shot put in Berlin and fling it out to 14.14 metres. It was a hell of a time to do a personal best. By the time I had won my 200 metres heat in 23.25 seconds, the overnight lead after the first day was up to 307 points. Even though there was still a day to go, Dobrynska patted me on the back after the 200 metres and said: 'You're the champ.'

I did not feel that way but that night I slept well. I usually do. By the time you leave the stadium, having had a bit of physio and some food, it is late. I don't talk to my parents in between, but I rang Andy and said, 'Not a bad day, then.' You just need a bit of reassurance, but I don't read the papers or the Internet. I don't want to see anything that might upset me or add to the pressure. So I am happy in my cocoon in my room.

The next day I knew it was mine to lose. The main problem was the heat. It was scorching and the girls were all struggling to stay cool. I grabbed an ice pack and started massaging my legs. I did not know that simple act caused panic attacks back home in Sheffield where Mum was watching. 'I thought you were injured,' she would later tell me. 'I was having a heart attack.'

The long jump was good enough. I cleared 6.29 metres and, while that was far from great, I was happy in the circumstances. After the javelin, with only the 800 metres to go, I was 171 points clear of the field. Dobrynska was down in fourth and Chernova in ninth.

I had an agonizing wait before the final event. I knew I had ten seconds to play with, but I was still worried. There was so much that could go wrong. At home I did not realize that my mum was getting just as wound up. My sister and dad were making such a lot of noise watching that it was getting on her nerves. So she went upstairs to watch on her own, in quiet if not exactly peace.

I knew I had to get to the front. I did not want to get tripped by anyone. I did not want to get barged or spiked or boxed. The gold medal was hanging there, tantalizingly close but still a world away. Or at least two minutes in the distance. Chell told me what I needed to do.

'Just run a steady pace,' he said. 'You've got a good cushion.'

'Okay,' I said.

We lined up. Under floodlights the bright blue track shimmered. And then we were off. I ran the first lap in just over a minute. That is way too fast. It is the sort of pace the specialist 800 metres runners might go. All over the place, from Chell in the stand to Mum and Dad at home, people were wondering what I was doing. I had a ten-yard lead and then the lactic acid started to kick in and I felt the raw pain of the 800 metres. Chell tells me I fear the event more than I need to. It's the reptilian side of my brain or something. Fight or flight. But I hated it then. The agony was intense but I knew I had only 300 metres to go. Then, coming off the last bend, Dobrynska overtook me and I thought, 'I'm not having that.' So I responded. Fight and flight. All those running sessions, all that hurt. I thought, 'These few seconds are why you did all that. It's so you can push harder than the rest. If you don't push now, all those sessions are wasted.' I came down the inside and won the race and the gold medal. The winning margin was 238 points. Jennifer Oeser was second. I collapsed on the track. It was over.

I was handed a flag by a pair of twins who are mad followers of British athletics. I draped myself in it and began the lap of honour. Believe me, it took a massive effort to get round again. Maybe that is why we were slow, which meant we were all held up at the top of the home straight because they were just about to run the 100 metres final. So I sat down and watched Usain Bolt run the fastest 100 metres ever seen. If you are going to be delayed by anything, then I suppose that's a pretty good reason. Anyway, it didn't take long.

We went into the mixed zone where you do the interviews with the TV, radio and press guys. Everybody was so pleased. I did my press conference and, as I came out of the room, Bolt walked in for his. He congratulated me and I did the same. Doc got a few pictures of us together. I have never seen them.

At home my mum had run down the stairs and was now joining Dad and Carmel in screaming the place down. I rang them twenty minutes afterwards for a quick chat. Then I rang the next day too. They were watching highlights of me on the TV and so Carmel just picked the phone off the hook and put it back down again without speaking. I tried again. The same thing. And again. Eventually my mum answered.

'Don't you want to speak to me or something?' I said.

She said they had gone to the shop because they had not got any champagne in beforehand. 'We got chicken and chips because we haven't eaten for two days,' Mum told me. In the corner shop my mum was trying to explain what had happened to Tony, the owner who has known me and Carmel since we were little. 'It hadn't sunk in,' she explained.

I went for a drink that night in an open-air bar outside the Olympic Stadium. Andy and his brothers were all there. It was late and there weren't many people around, but I was still draped in the Union Jack. I tried to take it all in – the win, the comeback and the fact that my lap of honour had been interrupted. People asked if I was annoyed by that. Of course not.

I did a lot of press afterwards. It was weird to think that nobody had been there to see me in places like Cleckheaton at the start of the year. Now people were asking me all sorts of questions, not all about sport. Some were about my looks. I found that embarrassing. I don't look in the mirror and think, 'Oh God yeah.' I don't think I'm anything special. Others speculated on how much money I would make, as if that was the most important thing.

I was looking forward to seeing my parents and Myla, my new Labrador puppy. 'I've no idea what it will be like,' I said. 'You're in a cocoon here. Usually, I can go out for a drink at home unbothered. It's only occasionally that someone gets a bit drunk and says, "Hey, you're that heptathlon girl." My parents say it's gone mad, but I don't know if I'm going to get a big welcome or just a couple of people clapping.' It turned out that there were lots of people when they held a civic reception for me, a highlight of which was receiving a Mulberry handbag from Sheffield City Council. They are a particular weakness of mine and that was the first of many I now own.

It got more surreal for us all after that. Journalists camped outside my mum and dad's house, and kept putting messages through the door. Dad had to escape and so he went to his allotment.

I got home and removed the champagne bottle that had stood on top of my fridge for a year. It had been given to me when I missed the Olympics, by Joe Rafferty, who worked for Adidas. I read the message written on it for the last time

Open this when you are world champion in 2009

and then I popped the cork.

7

REIGNING IN SPAIN

S port has a habit of giving with one hand and clobbering you with the other. I started 2010 in the form
of my life but then felt a problem in my foot. I
mentioned it to Chell.

'I don't mean to worry you but I've got a pain,' I told
him.

His face dropped. Then he dropped everything else
and we had it checked out straightaway. This time I went
for an MRI scan in Leeds and found that there was a
slight strain on the ligament that runs around the side
of the foot. It was my right foot, what you might term
the wrong foot.

The doctor told me the bones were fine, but the frustration wasn't. I had worked hard during the winter and
felt I was in the form of my life. In various events, I had
achieved eight personal bests in a month, as well as a

British indoor record in the 60 metres hurdles. In that race I beat Lolo Jones, the almost untouchable world indoor hurdles champion, in Glasgow. It is always satisfying to beat the specialists. Combined eventers are sometimes referred to as jacks of all trades, so it is nice to go against specialists and show we can be competitive. I had attempted the British high jump record in Glasgow too and think that may have been where the problem started. The next day it felt a bit tight, but I went on to have a really good week of training and was running good times. The tightness lingered, though, and now that I had a history, I knew I should have it checked out.

As a result I missed the trials for the World Indoor Championships and the Aviva Grand Prix event in Birmingham, but I did make it to the World Indoor Championships, which were held in March 2010 in Doha, Qatar – in the combined events, athletes are picked on form or past performances and so trials are never 'sudden death'. I found it an odd place and, even though we were indoors, the dry heat was awful. I was up against Hyleas Fountain, who had not been at the World Championships, and Dobrysnka was back in top form, so with another batch of training ruined by the foot problem, I had plenty of doubts going into the pentathlon.

However, it could scarcely have gone any better. I ended up 86 points clear of Dobrynska, broke Carolina Klüft's championship record and was four seconds short of breaking the eighteen-year-old world record of Irina Belova, which some say is tainted given that she failed a drug test the year after.

I was ecstatic to have backed up my performance in Berlin, and I told reporters, 'I've beaten them all now, here or in Berlin, and that's the nicest thing – to come back this year and prove I'm not a one-hit wonder.'

Chell likes to talk to the press and said people were making the 'extraordinary ordinary' by expecting a world record that 'Klüft had several bashes at and didn't achieve.' He was defensive like that, but I was just relieved because I hadn't done nearly as much as I had wanted to in training and had blown up in an 800 metres time-trial just before leaving.

The only downside to Qatar was that I was so dehydrated that I spent five hours trying to give a sample in doping. The only other girl in there was a hurdler. She was there when I went in and there when I left. She might still be there now. Chell sat with me for a bit, then Jane came in. It was boring and frustrating because all I wanted to do was celebrate.

It was around then that Charles van Commenee started saying he wanted me to move down to London. Lee Valley was going to be one of the national high performance centres and he felt that would be better for me to be based there. I could not understand that. I had won the world title and everything was working perfectly.

Moving to London would have been the very worst thing for me. I had a nice home in Yorkshire but they wanted me to go and live in an athlete's house, which would have been going back to university and living in halls. Charles said I would have everything I needed at the centre, but it wasn't just about that. Andy had a job in Sheffield and my family and friends were all there. I like to have separation in my life and do things outside of sport. He didn't get it. I don't like conflict, but if it is something that I am passionate about then I will put my foot down and argue until the sun comes down.

Eventually, he saw where I was coming from, but he still wanted me to move and tried to get Chell's job based down there to force it.

'I'm loyal to you,' Chell said. 'If you don't want to go then we don't.'

We didn't. I had never even competed in London and it would have been bad for me professionally and personally. I was world champion and I wanted to walk my dog with Hannah and have friends round for dinner. It was all so unnecessary.

The performances remained good. In May 2010, I went back to Götzis, in Austria. I told the media that I was not bothered about what had happened there before, but of course I was. Everything reminded me of how my world had caved in two years earlier – the mountains, the physio room, the woman in heels in the town hall pointing out how small I was. However, I had no problems this time other than the black sky and thunderous rain. The top girls were there and Chernova really stuck at me, trimming my lead to 77 points going into the final event, but I responded and won the 800 metres.

There had been a lot of talk of me breaking Denise Lewis's British record beforehand. It had stood at 6831 points since 2000. 'People talk about Denise's record but you can't think beyond one event,' I told a group of journalists. 'Get that wrong and it messes up the whole thing and that's when it's hard. You take a few minutes for self-pity, have a little cry and then try to put it into perspective.'

When did I cry during a heptathlon, I was asked? 'Osaka,' I said immediately. 'Close to tears, anyway. You work so hard to make everything right and then something goes wrong and you want to kick yourself and disappear.' I thought about just how many tears I had shed, from Beijing to the boiler breaking down, and smiled.

The issue of doping came up again. I said I could not understand why anyone would do it. The reporter suggested money, fame or jealousy? 'But is it worth the risk of people thinking you're a disgrace, let alone the health issues?' I said. 'Anyway, my family would kill me.'

Then, with everything going smoothly, came another clobbering. The ankle problem I had at the start of the year was replaced by a major scare just before the European

Championships in Barcelona. It started after a training session in Leeds. I felt a bit faint and just thought I was probably a bit dehydrated and so I sat down, drank something and felt okay to drive home. I trained the next day and thought nothing of it. I went home to get ready to go out for a friend's birthday and then the whole room started to spin. It was frightening. I tried to stand up, but that made it worse, the room spun quicker and I felt sick. I couldn't even move my head from one side to another. I wondered what was going on; I was panicking. I lay down on the bed and rang Andy.

'Can you come home? There's something's wrong with me.'

The EIS doctor, Richard Higgins, came out and said it was probably a virus that was affecting my inner ear. He prescribed some tablets and said that my balance would improve. Sure enough it did for a few days, but then I had another attack and it was back to square one. You start to imagine the worst in situations like that, especially after I went back to Google. I read about people who had the same thing and could never drive again. Before long I was wondering if my career was over again. The latest dizzy spell was far worse than the others. It was like being spun around endless times. I saw Richard Higgins and he said I should see an ear, nose and throat specialist. I went along and the specialist said there were two options. The first was to take a course of tablets for three weeks, with the side effects of feeling sick and having headaches, or I could try the Epley manoeuvre.

I did not know what it was but I did know that it sounded vaguely painful.

'It could clear it up within a day,' he said.

'Great.'

'Or it could make it worse.'

I often think that doctors hand out medication a bit too freely and so, having dragged Andy along with me to the specialist, I said I thought I should try the Epley manoeuvre. That was when the doctor got behind me, grasped my head and jerked it gently one way at 45 degrees. Then he did it the other way 90 degrees.

A few days later I went for a brain scan. They are always anxious times as you wonder what on earth they might find in there. I hoped for the best and feared the worst. I began to worry that I might have a brain tumour. It took me back to the scan I'd had on my injured foot two years before. I remembered how everybody had told me it would be all right and there was nothing to worry about, only for the cold, hard facts of an X-ray to prove them all wrong. It was the same this time.

'Don't worry,' everybody said. 'It will be nothing.'

This time they were right. I got the all-clear and felt a huge, unseen burden lift. I asked the consultant what could have been the cause.

'There could be any number of reasons,' he said.

'Like what?'

'Well, have you been under any stress lately?'

Stressed! As an athlete you are always stressed. You win a competition but quickly look to the next one. The goalposts are constantly shifting. The pressure close to a major event is huge. Most of it is internal pressure you put on yourself to turn all the hard work into your best, but there was growing external pressure too, from the public, the sponsors and the media. I had made it look quite easy in Berlin and that was a curse really, because this was really very hard.

So I might have been stressed without even knowing it. For years the American 400 metres runner, Sanya Richards-Ross, thought she was suffering from a condition called Behçet's Disease that left her with mouth ulcers and skin lesions. It sounded horrible and was brought on by stress. Although she later said she had been mis-diagnosed, there is no doubt stress can be a debilitating thing for an athlete, at the same time as having positive benefits in some ways.

I had missed three weeks and, when I was then made the team captain for the Europeans, my stress levels rose even higher. I am proud to represent Great Britain, but I am not a confident person. I felt it would be rude and ungrateful to turn down the offer, but the thought of having to give a team speech, as is the tradition, kept me up at night. Part of me thought that it would be good to put myself out of my comfort zone, but I didn't enjoy the experience at all.

A year on from Berlin and we were heading to another Olympic Stadium. The capacity had been reduced considerably since then and the football club that used to play there, Espanyol, had moved out. At some sessions there were big spaces on the terraces, but I still felt those same echoes of the past swirling around on the wind. Linford Christie was invited by Charles van Commenee to give us a speech. He actually read out a poem about his own experiences of winning the Olympic 100 metres gold in Barcelona back in 1992.

I was far too young to remember any of that, but I was moved by his poem. It was short and quite funny. Then he read out another one, titled 'Desiderata', by the American poet Max Ehrmann. It ended with the lines: *'With all its sham, drudgery, and broken dreams/It is still a beautiful world/Be cheerful/Strive to be happy . . .'*

I cannot say that I am a particular fan of poetry, but with Linford reading that out, in the vicinity of the Olympic Stadium, and with all of us preparing to compete, it touched a nerve. It also made me feel even more nervous when I had to give my speech. I don't think it would win any prizes, but I spoke about my injuries and making the most of opportunities. Some people are naturally better at being captain. Dai Greene would lead the team in London and was great. Goldie Sayers was another good one, a lovely person who put individual notes under all our doors before one competition. For me, the role was a burden.

The captaincy added to my media commitments ahead of the Europeans, and I was aware that my profile was rising, not least when Charles said I would be the only athlete judged a failure if I did not win gold in Spain.

'I will still be young in 2012, only twenty-six, but you have a shelf life in the heptathlon,' I told *The Times* that day in Barcelona. 'The body can only take so much. It's all the training no one sees. Eventually, the body says it's had enough. I don't know whether that will be after 2012, and what happens afterwards also depends on whether I've achieved everything I've wanted to. I just want to feel satisfied. I think you know when that is.'

My shelf life as the 'Leader', the bib they give to the heptathlete who heads the rankings after each event, was threatened in Barcelona. Dobrynska had turned up in great shape and I expected it to be close. In the end it came down to a matter of inches.

The nerves and stress were bubbling before the hurdles. Chernova was one of two girls to false-start in my heat. It meant that anyone else false-starting would be disqualified and out of the running. In those circumstances you tell yourself to stay in the blocks. Don't go until the gun. Sometimes, though, as I would find out to my cost in the future, your subconscious takes over.

I got out fast, was smooth over the hurdles and clocked 12.95 seconds. It was a good start and I backed it up with 1.89 metres in the high jump. It had been raining that morning so I was happy enough, but Dobrynska was fighting hard. She is far more powerful in the shot and so my lead was trimmed to just 11 points after three events. Whereas many events are seriously weakened at the Europeans because of the lack of American and Caribbean athletes, the heptathlon was a line-up of all the top girls, with the exception of Fountain. It was hard, fast and gruelling. I made up more points in the 200 metres, clocking 23.21 seconds, but I knew Dobrynska could strike back at me in the long jump and javelin. It had never been closer.

It was the same on day two. I was still unconvinced by my long jump. Everyone told me that I should be able to jump much further because of my speed on the runway, but it just was not happening. Somewhere in me, though, is that competitive gene, the attention-seeking bit that thrives on the pressure and the big stage. Dobrynska laid down a marker by jumping a season's best of 6.56 metres, but I responded with 6.43 metres on my last jump. The damage had been limited. I'd done the same in the shot put, saving the best until last, all those sessions with John and the wagers struck for chocolate paying off.

Dobrynska was not giving up, though. She managed her best-ever javelin throw, 49.25 metres, to keep snapping away at my heels. I also threw better than ever, reaching 46.71 metres, and when the scores were totted up and sums done, I basically knew she had to beat me by two seconds in the 800 metres. My parents had come out to Spain and this was the first major championships they had been to. Andy was also there and so was Carmel, who watched my javelin and swiftly brought me back down to earth by saying: 'Blimey, you can actually throw now.'

I could have tucked in behind Dobrynska in the 800 metres and tracked her, making sure the gap never grew into a defeat, or I could have gone out and run hard from the front. I chose the latter. It's the way I like to run. I am small and don't want to get beaten up. I hit the front and, instead, Dobrynska tracked me. I could see her on the big screen. On the penultimate bend she made her move and edged past me. I was not having that and responded. I knew that I needed to run 2 minutes 9.59 seconds to break Denise's British record at last. I saw off Dobrynska and crossed the line in 2.10.18. The winning margin was 45 points which equates to about three inches in the long jump. It had been a competition of broad scope and fine margins.

It felt amazing. I was the world and European champion. There was only one thing missing now, and the talk of London increased even though it was two years away. I joined up with Andy, my family, and the team and went down Las Ramblas. It was late and there were a dozen of us so it was hard to get in anywhere. We ended up outside a tapas bar but they said it was full. I was tired, hungry and felt annihilated. A TV screen hung on a wall inside and it flashed to my 800 metres. Andy started pointing at me.

'That's her, it's her,' he said.

The man looked at the screen and then at me. He paused for a second while he made the connection.

'Come in,' he said.

It wasn't the only door that would be opened on the back of a gold medal.

8

THE BIG TIME

I t was a letter I got at the end of 2010 that showed me there is another, less welcome side to being in the public eye. I was one of many athletes who chose not to go to the Commonwealth Games, staged in Delhi in October 2010. The reason was simple. They were being held far too late in the year. My year is built around the major summer championships and training blocks are geared to that, so travelling to India in October was going to throw everything out of synch.

There were all sorts of problems in the build-up to Delhi and some people were portrayed as cowards for not competing there. For me, though, it had nothing to do with security, dengue fever, dodgy safety certificates or falling footbridges. It was just bad timing.

One man did not see it that way. He sent me a very long letter explaining how disappointed he was and how

I was letting the whole country down. How could I turn down the opportunity to represent my country? He was clearly someone who would die for England and he raged on. 'I will not be supporting you in 2012,' he concluded. I found that upsetting.

There have been other messages, including a few about death. One man said he wanted to take Myla out for a walk and spoke about us walking on a beach and dying together. That got reported to the police. There are others that are a bit creepy. Generally, I try to take them lightly and with a bit of humour, but Andy gets worried. There can also be a few intense and, at times, rather creepy people around the tracks too. Maybe it is the fact that it's a sport where women do not wear a great deal. I find that the best policy is to be respectful and polite wherever possible, while Jane generally tried to keep anything odd away from me.

Generally, though, I get nice letters. After Berlin I received lots of lovely messages from kids addressed simply to 'Jessica Ennis, World Champion'. There would be autograph requests and homemade cards. I was touched.

People are usually nice and the opportunities that winning the world and European titles brought were beyond a Sheffield schoolgirl's dreams. So when Adidas asked Jane if I would like to go to Los Angeles to do a photo-shoot with David Beckham, she said yes immediately and added that she would need to come too.

Andy also came along as chaperone and we flew out to a lovely boutique hotel, the Sunset Marquis in West Hollywood. It was a haven for proper stars rather than a Yorkshire heptathlete. In one corner sat Usher, the R&B megastar, flanked by huge bodyguards. I said hello and was unashamedly starry-eyed. Apparently, there was a recording studio at the hotel and Cheryl Cole was also staying there.

On the day of the shoot we were driven up into the Hollywood hills to a huge glass-fronted mansion that looked out over the city. I sat in a room with David Beckham's hair and make-up people and then I did my shoot. There was an air of expectancy as we awaited his arrival. When he did come, he politely shook everyone's hand and asked how we were. He had an aura and I could feel everyone staring at him, but I imagine he is used to it. We did some pictures together and he showed me his scar from his Achilles injury. He was as nice and grounded as anyone you'll meet. His music was playing in the house through his iPod. When a song came on that had some swearing in it, he rushed in and told someone to change it because his kids were around. I noticed how his kids tore all over the grounds, pursued by bodyguards, and could not imagine how he managed to live like that and remain so normal. I had experienced it on a tiny scale, but he could not go anywhere in the world without someone checking the house and watching over his kids.

I thought it must be a weird life, but he was so approachable and normal and I liked him a lot. Some celebrities are only interested in their own worlds, but he asked me about training and injuries and then told me he wanted more kids. If I'd been a journalist it would have been a world exclusive, and I remember thinking how open he had been. I have since grown to realize that sportspeople have a real respect for one another and a mutual trust.

With the gold medals came some fantastic sponsorship opportunities, particularly with the Olympic ones, and I began to do more photo-shoots. One of the first was at Forgemasters, the steelworks just down the road from where I train. The theme was simple enough, me being forged of Sheffield steel, but the shoot was more problematic. Obviously, it was blindingly hot in there and one man had the task of literally making sparks fly as the camera clicked. It was a normal day's work for the men there, and so it was slightly odd to be standing there in a fairly skimpy athletics kit, with a throng of men in goggles looking on. As the sparks flew I thought, 'This is a bit close', and it was not the safest environment for a wannabe Olympic athlete, with metal strips lying around the floor, but the pictures were great.

If Chell would have cringed at that one, he would have had kittens when I was driven out into the Derbyshire countryside to do some pictures for *Vogue*. The idea for this one was for me to wear a lovely white dress and heels and stand on a rocky outcrop overlooking a valley. It sounded simple enough, but what the pictures did not show was that I was literally on the edge of a sheer drop and it was very windy.

'I'm not really comfortable with this,' I said, but I did it anyway, despite the wind that was whipping up and the crew of lighting men and assistants who were gathered around the edge to catch me if I fell. Nobody told Chell, of course, and the pictures were suitably dramatic.

I am like a lot of women in that I love fashion and being pampered, although glamour shoots can sometimes be a bit of a contradiction in terms. When I did a shoot for *Marie Claire*, the very vivacious and absolutely lovely American photographer spent his time saying, 'Oh my God, darling', before the shoot culminated in me leaning over a hurdle and a bunch of people chucking bottles of water at me. I loved the pictures but was soaking wet and had to get the train back north to Sheffield with my hair dripping. Another time I did a shoot for *Stylist* magazine. This one involved having red, white and blue powder paint blown in my face through straws. I ended up with powder in my ears and up my nose and got plenty of stares from people who thought my hair was caked in blood as I rushed for another train. The cover would be amazing, though, and so I felt it had been worth it.

I think it's important to try new things and take advantage of opportunities, but I never took my eye off the prize. I also have limits. I did some sexier shots for *GQ* magazine, wearing some hot-pants and pouting. My mum rang me when she saw them. 'Young lady, you didn't tell me about that, did you?' Andy gets the mickey taken out of him at work for it, but I would never do topless or nude pictures or even be body-painted. That is where I draw the line. I have really enjoyed this side of my life. Having make-up artists and stylists dress me and famed photographers shoot me for ad campaigns or magazines is the thing that many girls dream of, and is a far cry from traipsing around sweaty sports centres in a tracksuit.

Life was certainly changing and I was engaged by now. That happened on Christmas Eve. Normally we go to the local pub, the Robin Hood, on Christmas Eve, but this time we were off to an Italian restaurant. Andy and I had spoken about marriage but I had no inkling that anything was happening when he called me into our front room and asked me to sit down. I thought that was odd and then realized what was happening, but tempered the excitement by thinking he could not possibly have a ring. He spoke a bit about how we had been seeing each other for a long time now and I thought, 'This is it.' By the time he got down on one knee I could tell how nervous he was, but I was so happy. We called Mum and Carmel who both screamed their consent down the phone. Dad already knew because Andy had asked to see him the day before and asked his permission. I think

Dad was relieved when that was all he wanted. It made for a great Christmas and made up for the time Andy had got a bit worse for wear, danced on the living-room table and fallen headfirst into the Christmas tree, putting a huge dent in the present I had bought for Grandad and lovingly wrapped.

There was never any question of getting married before the Olympics. I could not fully enjoy it beforehand because I had this big weight looming over everything. I thought the dream would be to win the Olympics and then have time to plan the wedding. Chell came around and I expected him to tell me straightaway that the wedding was off until after London, but he gave me a congratulations card and seemed very happy for us.

It was a good start to the year, but things rarely stayed smooth for long. I started the 2011 season at the Northern Athletics Indoor Championships at the EIS in Sheffield. A week later I clocked 8.03 seconds for the 60 metres hurdles and then dropped that time to 7.97 seconds at the Aviva International in Glasgow. It was a light start to the year, the phoney war if you like, as I targeted the European Indoor Championships in Paris in March.

The Olympic schedule was released that February. Chell had had some discussions about organizing the schedule so that I could do the hurdles as well as the heptathlon. I have always liked the hurdles more than any other single event, and sometimes watch the specialists turn up, run their race and go home with a degree of envy. It looks so simple and, when your body is crying out in pain the day after doing seven events, very tempting. However, the schedule only had one day between the end of the heptathlon and the hurdles heats and so I felt it was too little recovery time. It was never really on my radar from that moment.

I went back to the EIS for the European trials. I had planned to do a few events, but only got through the shot put, my worst of the year, and the high jump before I knew something was wrong. UK Athletics issued a press release saying it was just precautionary and we thought it was, but the pain in the Achilles would fester on and refuse to go away. Before long I accepted I would have to pull out of Paris. The UKA doctor thought I had torn my calf and that the blood was dripping down and pooling near the Achilles. The pain was not too bad and I felt I could have gone to France if my life depended on it, but I was looking at the bigger picture.

I could not run or jump. Hurdling was out. I was stressing now because it kept nagging away. I did my rehab, as I'd grown used to under Ali, but there was confusion about what was wrong. I went to London to see an Achilles specialist and he did an ultrasound. He told me that the problem was the plantaris tendon that runs alongside the Achilles. He said that not everyone had it and, basically, we had evolved and it was now redundant. It was like the appendix. He suggested he went in and snipped it.

The talk of operations scared me because I'd never had one. How will I heal? What if it gets infected? What if the doctor's wrong? I was against it and, luckily, Chell, Derry and Ali felt the same way. It's easy to accept what doctors say unquestioningly, but we decided to do it our way.

Ali did lots of work on the calf and I did all I was told, but the weeks continued to tick by with little progress. For someone who hates missing even a single session that was hard. Desperate times called for desperate measures and so I tried cryotherapy. That meant I had to go to Champneys Tring health resort and enter an ice chamber where temperatures are kept at minus 135°C to aid blood circulation. After a minute in there I went into a second chamber, which was a steady minus 90°C, for a couple more.

It felt like the indoor season was causing me problems and I always seemed to come away with something. I heard a story about another girl who had the same issue. She had the operation and got back to the top of her game very quickly. I wondered if I should have done the same. In all I had seven weeks out, during which time I flew to Orlando for an Adidas shoot and was so frustrated to watch the likes of Tyson Gay, the top American sprinter, doing his track sessions, while I had a bunch of boring rehab exercises to do in the gym. I was cranky and impatient at not being able to run and, for me, seven weeks seemed a lifetime. Later Chell told me that the girl who'd had the operation had broken down with a ruptured Achilles. I felt very relieved that I had not chosen the same route.

I made my comeback in May 2011, three months after I had last performed. I went to the Great City Games in Manchester, an outdoors event where they erect a track down Deansgate, the main thoroughfare in the city centre, and let you run by the shops and punters. It is novel but a good way of trying to get more people into the sport, although I had no such worthy aims when I turned up. I just wanted to prove to myself that I was going to be able to make it to Götzis in a fortnight, because I desperately needed to do a heptathlon before the World Championships, which were being held in Daegu in South Korea and beginning in August.

It was grey and miserable in Manchester, but I got through. I was happy with my 100 metres hurdles time of 12.88 seconds, my fourth fastest, and less so with my 150 metres, but I was in one piece. 'She should have got well and truly spanked given the lack of training,' Chell said to the media.

It was a gamble going to Götzis with barely six weeks' training done. Because I'd been planning an indoor season, where there is no javelin, and then got injured,

I'd had little time to work on that event. I had also become something of a dream freak in the meantime. I had one and looked up the meaning in my book and it seemed really significant. It said if you dream this, then you will never achieve your goal. There was a caveat, though, and it said if it also involved something specific, like a flower with a petal missing, which it did, then you'd work hard and get everything you want. Sometimes I felt as if I was grasping at straws.

Everybody was in Götzis in May. It was the dry-run before Daegu where I would put my world title on the line. I was worried and anxious, but I actually felt in brilliant running shape. Maybe sometimes you need a break and, when you are an athlete, you don't allow yourself that. I sat in my small hotel room, with a box of Jaffa cakes, box set of *Grey's Anatomy* and the tube holding my javelins, and counted down.

For once the fears were unfounded and Götzis was brilliant for me. 'She'll have a face like a slapped backside,' Chell said cheerily to the media guys as he came down to greet me after the javelin on day two. I knew I could have thrown better, but 43.83 metres was okay and I was happy. I was not worried about Denise's British record today. The other girls were struggling and, by the time I edged out Jessica Zelinka in the 800 metres, clocking a personal best of 2 minutes 8.46 seconds, I was struggling to contain my emotions. I had scored 6790 points, my second-best tally, and had beaten the rest by 251 points. I knew that Daegu was likely to be different, but knowing that Dobrynska had only been 45 points behind me the last time we met, I had every reason to be cheerful.

It had been a huge weekend. I knew that, even with minimal training, I could get myself into peak running shape and that might be good enough to carry me through. Suddenly, everything felt like it was back on track.

My journey into the surreal reached a new peak with the news that I had got an MBE in the Queen's Birthday honours. Deep down I thought things like that did not happen to people like me. I was just Jessica Ennis, the same woman from Yorkshire I had always been, with the same friends, same motivations and same beliefs. But I also know that there was now another Jessica Ennis, the one on the billboards, the TV and, soon, at Buckingham Palace.

There was also a Jessica Ennis in Madame Tussauds. I had been shocked when Suzi told me they wanted to do a waxwork of me. I'd never been, but had obviously heard of the place, so I went down and did a sitting. It was a fascinating if painstaking process. I had to sit for ages while they took photographs of me from every angle, slowly turning me round on a spinning board, and taking hundreds of measurements. I was surprised as I had expected them to take a cast of my face, but they did everything from their own calculations and expert eye. They then cut a lock of hair to get a sample, gauged my teeth colour on a white board and matched my eyes to a chart.

Some time later, when I was down in London doing a photo-shoot at a studio, they said they would bring my head along. It was an unnerving experience, like the film *Seven* with Gwyneth Paltrow's severed head turning up in a box. I felt uneasy when someone at the shoot said: 'Your head is here.' Then they came in and lifted the clay face from the cardboard container. I thought this is brilliantly freaky. The next time I saw it was the night before the unveiling. Andy and I arrived late and there were just a couple of people from Madame Tussauds there. They touched up the colouring and added a few freckles. It was dark and quiet and I could feel hundreds of glass eyes on me. We got taken on a personal tour after that, although I gave the Chambers of Horrors a miss and remember Bruce Willis's eyes seemed to follow me everywhere. I told them to stick me next to David Beckham and was happy to get out.

9

THE WHEELS
COME OFF

Andy would leave early for work leaving me to wake up slowly. I would take Myla for a walk and then stumble out of the house at about 9 a.m., fuelled by toast or cereal. Chell had not wanted us to get Myla because he thought she would be a distraction. She was, but in a nice way. Yes, I had to take a lot of phone calls from people saying, 'Your dog is in our garden', and, yes, I was mortally embarrassed by her behaviour at the obedience classes, a contradiction in terms as it turned out, but she was therapy when I was getting back on my feet. Even if it meant pursuing her down the street in my PJs, or crying as she gnawed her way through the radiator pipes, she was the nicest sort of distraction.

According to Chell's colour chart, I was green and need a plan. That was why I worked six days a week at seven events for one big championship a year. It's risky when your season comes down to two days, but I don't know how footballers can be competitive every week. My week was designed to get me ready for those two days, this time at the World Championships. I left Götzis and carried on working away, building up the unseen gains that I hoped would see me through. They were hellish weeks that went like this.

MONDAY

Another week would start for me with an 800 metres running session in the morning and my hurdles drills. Then I did some circuits and throwing. We looked at videos to analyse what I was doing wrong. There was always something. The shot was something we had studied in detail, going over videos of my action, and seeing how I glide across the circle. Chell would demonstrate, I would laugh and somehow it would come together. Then I'd finish the day with more violent treatment from Derry.

TUESDAY

Javelin day. I drove up to Leeds to do my weekly session with Mick. My javelin had come on leaps and bounds.

In heptathlon you will always have favourite events, but I knew I could not afford any bad ones. The bad ones had to be average, the standards shifted.

I would see Ali in Leeds too. She did the same assessment at the start of each session, making me stand up and bend over, while she checked to see if my pelvis was off line or if there were any displacements.

WEDNESDAY

This was my long-jump day at Loughborough. Bricey the biomechanist helped Chell analyse my speed and the angle of take-off. We freeze-framed the videos but it was still a very difficult event for me. It had been a trial to change my take-off foot, but in a way it simplified things. I now had one foot for high jump and one for long jump. My brain could work with that. I took lunch with some other athletes. Steve Lewis, the pole-vaulter, was usually there. We came up through the ranks together, so there was a lot of banter. The pole-vaulters are crazy and I remember one, Nick Buckfield, landing on the pole and almost having an enema. It was way too dangerous for me. After lunch I went back to Sheffield for a weights session.

THURSDAY

My day off. I could switch off from sport. I didn't usually look up my rivals on the Internet to see how they are doing. My friends are not particularly sporty and I would try to catch up with them. It was also the day to get any commercial commitments done.

FRIDAY

Friday was a technical morning doing hurdles and high jump. Chell would have his laptop computer out and spreadsheets showing comparisons for the past four years. I liked that because it drove me on to know I was running faster at this point in 2007. He'd tell me he made me, that I'd be nothing without him. I would try to laugh it off or ignore him.

The hurdles is one of my best events, but there is always room for improvement. Then I'd have another shot-put session in the afternoon, some plyometrics to help make me more explosive and then a weights session. I'm not bad in the gym. I'm small but I can lift quite a bit over my bodyweight.

SATURDAY

I would start off with another javelin session with Mick.
I'd got used to not having weekends. There were plenty
of other people in the same boat and at least I always
have a goal. Daegu was now occupying all my time. I had
to get it right. If I could defend my title there, I would
be set up for London and 2012. I wanted to keep this
winning streak going and underline my ability. I wanted
the other girls to know how badly I wanted this.

SUNDAY

I didn't have a regular psychologist, although we would
talk to Pete Lindsay at times. I thought they were good
but sometimes I wondered whether you go because you
have a problem or to create one. It was possible to overcomplicate it. On Sunday I'd think about everyone else
getting over their Saturday nights and consider that my
weekend was rubbish. So I'd leave the house feeling utterly
miserable. It was also a hard, long day with lots of weights
and running. I'd do a ten-minute jog as a warm-up and
run. I would do something like 250 metres, rest for three
minutes and then 240 metres and so on. I've done a lot
of work with physiologists to find out what are the best

sessions for me. You might think a long run would be good for the 800 metres but it's not. Sometimes I'd do an 800 metres time-trial but generally I would not run for more than 350 metres at a time. The best thing is 200 and 300-metre repetitions with little recovery time so you get the lactic acid in your legs and there's no time to shift it before you go again. I could be very grumpy when I'm tired and this stuff hurts. Then it would be Monday again, a week closer to Daegu and the next huge test.

Another Monday turned to Tuesday and the weeks ticked by. It was now less than a year to the Olympic Games and every countdown had been marked in the media – 1,000 days, two years, 500 days, one year, tick-tock. The truth is I was more concerned with the moment and Daegu. London was the endgame but you had to put yourself in a position to win it and that would be decided now. I would drive past five big posters of me on advertising hoardings on the way to training. It was still hard to take in. One night I was driving to a chip shop and was about to go in when I saw the huge Powerade ad hanging outside. There I was, supposedly sweating after a hard session, clad in Lycra and selling good health. I thought, 'God, I can't go in now', and drove on to Sainsbury's instead. Later Chell had his picture taken next to that poster while tucking into a bag of chips. I had people telling me they could see me from their bedroom window. Carmel came back from a trip and said: 'Blimey, she's even big in Birmingham.' It was growing, but I had to back it all up with results. The pressure to defend my world title was raised with every billboard.

My warm-up for Daegu finished on a good note with a PB of 12.79 seconds in the 100 metres hurdles at Loughborough. That put me second on the UK all-time list, ahead of Angie Thorp, who had been the long-term British record-holder until her mark had been beaten by Tiffany Porter earlier that summer. Tiffany had been receiving a lot of flak as one of the so-called 'plastic Brits', athletes who had recently joined the British team from different countries. Tiffany grew up in America but she had a British passport. That was the end of the story for me. It's not as if they give them away.

Before I flew out to South Korea, Ali asked me if I was excited. I thought about it for a while and realized I never get excited before big competitions. It's more a feeling of mounting nervousness and anxiety as the entire year comes down to two days.

The weather in the holding camp in Ulsan had been awful and so we were expecting rain when we got to Daegu, but it turned out to be brighter than we'd hoped for. In some respects. Anyway – the event had already got off to a dramatic start when, on the second night, the eve of my competition, Usain Bolt false-started his way out of the 100 metres final. It caused a furore, with calls for rule changes and talk of thousands of people being short-changed, but I have always been one to stick to the rules. Mum and Carmel and others were the kind of people who might push them, but I believed they were there to be adhered to. Bolt had broken the rules so that was hard but fair. Mo Farah had been yards from winning the 10,000 metres title too, but was overhauled in the final strides. He had a look of almost terror on his face as he crossed the line for a silver medal. It was a great achievement but I knew it was not what he wanted.

The next morning, Monday 29 August, it was my turn. I was in the first heat, in lane two, flanked by Hyleas Fountain and Jessica Zelinka, both good hurdlers. Before the first event you start to think, 'Don't fall over', 'Don't false start'. Then I banish that negativity. I think dos, not don'ts. I felt good and was running well, shown by my time in Loughborough. Just repeat that and I would be in good shape, but in the hurdles there is a lot that can go wrong and my timing was ever so slightly out, a small mistake with big consequences. I clattered into a couple of hurdles and it knocked me off my pace. I was really annoyed and crossed the line seething with frustration at not having made the most of an opportunity. Fountain won the heat and I was second in 12.94 seconds. Dobrynska and Chernova both set personal bests in their heats. Already, it looked as if it was going to be tougher than ever.

Doc was there and looked at my knee. It hurt really badly, but he put a Voltarol patch on it and I was not too worried at that point. People often limp through the heptathlon, with their bodies falling apart and patched up by tape and bandages.

But the high jump was worse and did not flow at all. Maybe the knee played a part. I needed two attempts to get over even 1.80 metres. It was the same at 1.83 metres. By 1.86 metres, my minimum requirement, I was struggling. I grimaced as I felt the bar falling on my first two attempts. I had one more left and already I could see the wheels falling off. Chernova pulled out a season's best of 1.83 metres on her last attempt at that height, but that was as far as both she and Dobrynska got. I clipped the bar twice and then squeaked over 1.86 metres. It meant that Fountain led after two events with me second and Chernova third.

I went back to the combined events room in the stadium. This is a room where the girls can all stay if they want. Everyone has their own section. Sometimes they are screened off because nobody wants to let anyone else see if they are injured. If you see someone covered in strapping or having rigorous physio then you know they are struggling. I got back and was quite teary. The bruise on my knee had spread and it was darkening but worse was that I had hurt my ankle in one of my final jumps in the high jump and that was giving me the problem. It hurt to walk and I had five events left. I thought I was going to have to pull out, but Chell tried to lift me and put a positive spin on it.

'You'll be fine. There's a gap in the day now. Let's ice it and get some food.'

I was not convinced. I had an anti-inflammatory tablet and, although it was a bit sore, I went back out in the afternoon and threw a personal best of 14.67 metres in the shot put. That put me into the lead but Dobrynska looked strong and her 16.14 metres lifted her into third place, with Chernova dropping down to sixth, some 128 points adrift.

The 200 metres came just after the last of the 400 metres semi-finals, where Oscar Pistorius, the double amputee and Paralympic star, received a huge roar from the crowd as he made history. I did not notice. I was fully concentrated on me. There was a strong headwind so times were never going to be stunning, but I clocked 23.27 seconds to be the fastest woman in the competition. Chernova had been in the same heat and pushed me hard. She ran a personal best of 23.50 seconds and was delighted. She was up to second place after the first day.

I had mixed feelings. I was sorry not to have maximized my strong events and had my two problem ones ahead, but I was in the lead and with a healthy points advantage. I had beaten Chernova in all four events and the ankle did not seem too bad. It was around midnight when I got back to the village, but I went to sleep quickly, walking through the next day in my mind.

It was early morning when we made it to the stadium. There were not many people in for the morning session but it did not matter. I knew we had rebuilt the long jump and that I was capable of more. I had seen the proof on Bricey's laptop. I tore down the runway, tried not to think too much and reached. It is always a leap of faith. The opener was measured at 6.27 metres, which was not great, but not a disaster either. Chernova was jumping in the same pool and she started with 6.38 metres and then put in a big 6.61 metres. This was where she knew she could make inroads on my lead, but I responded with a personal best of 6.51 metres. All that fear and anticipation was suddenly replaced with relief I was 118 points clear of her. I was confident I could beat her if I had to in the 800 metres so it would all come down to the javelin.

In truth, I was not happy with my javelin going into the World Championships. The injury had meant I had lost a lot of technical work and I had been inconsistent all year. I just needed today to be one of the good days. They had split us into two groups for the event, with all the big hitters in the first one. I was annoyed by that. I am the sort of athlete who responds to other people's performances, but I had to suffer and watch as Chernova launched her javelin a huge 52.95 metres in the first group and then gave out a roar of effort and delight as it sailed into the crisp blue sky.

The pressure was now on. It was me and her now. She was ten inches taller and in the shape of her life; I had missed training and began to feel the walls closing in. I knew I was capable of throwing 45 metres and that would make it close going into the final event. The warm-up was okay. I pinged a couple to the 45 metres mark. I just needed to do it again. One shot. On the first one I bounced up, slipped and managed barely 38 metres. That was a disaster. There was a re-laid bit of track on the runway and if you didn't put your heel down properly then you could slip. I was tentative on the second one because I did not want to ruin the whole throw. It flopped at 39.95 metres. Now the pressure really was on, but I had been here before and pulled out jumps and throws when I needed to. All those wagers struck with John and Chell in the EIS had served me well. But not this time. I stuttered to the line and watched in horror as the javelin turned prematurely and flopped.

Anger, frustration, horror. They boiled over. I felt as though the odds were stacked against me. I had been injured in 2008 and now again this year. I felt it was not supposed to be. I walked back and Darren Campbell, the sprinter working for BBC Radio, collared me.

'It's not over yet, Jess.'

I knew, though. I knew in my heart. I went over to find Chell to find out what I needed to do in the 800 metres. He looked at me and his face said it more than the words. Somewhere deep down I had been thinking that maybe, just maybe, I could run an astonishing 800 metres and keep hold of the title. Then he told me the lead was 133 points. Chernova had made up 251 points in one event. The bottom line was I needed to beat her by nine seconds over two laps. It was gone – the nearest thing to impossible.

I went back to the combined events room and was trying as hard as I could not to cry. It was there that I could see Chell was close to tears too. It was the first time I had seen him like that and I could tell how much it had got to him. We were really in this together.

It was a few hours until the 800 metres. I lay on the physio bed and listened to some music. It was something mellow, not wrist-slashing stuff, but not upbeat. Eventually, the time came. We walked into the stadium for the final heat of the 800 metres, the one with all the leading contenders in it.

I was on the inside lane. Nine seconds. There was only one way to run that. Go for broke and try to break Chernova, hoping that I did not die in the last 200 metres and end up squandering the silver medal too. Nine seconds.

The gun. I went off fast, passing 200 metres in just

over 28 seconds. By the bell I was clear of her. I looked up at the huge scoreboard to see where Chernova was. She was tracking me in the knowledge that she just had to stay within nine seconds. I piled it on during the second lap. The gap increased down the back straight and, for a few fleeting moments, the impossible seemed plausible, but then I began to feel pain like never before. Karolina Tyminska, the best 800 metres runner in the field, came past me. I tried to hang on, but Chernova had run a good race where I could not afford to be sensible. I beat her over the line but the huge roar I heard from behind me showed she was too close to me. The personal best of 2 minutes 7.81 seconds was no consolation. I had lost.

I felt distraught but managed to smile and congratulate her. To be fair, she was in amazing shape and had put everything together. Her tally of 6880 points topped anything I'd ever done. But going on that lap of honour with the other girls was one of the hardest things I'd ever done, because I just wanted to go and lock myself behind a closed door and be miserable.

The press guys asked Chell whether I would come back. 'I think she already has,' he said. 'It would have been very easy for her to sit here and take silver and go home, but she put it all on the line. I respect her a lot for that.' He knew how much it hurt, though, and was not about to pretend this year did not matter because of 2012. 'That's pretty much rubbish. I'm sure Alex Ferguson doesn't say, "I want to lose the Premier League this year and win it next year when it's more important."'

He was right. I gave some interviews and said that it was not about this year, that it was all about 2012, but they were just words. It kills you. In the official press conference one journalist asked how it felt to have lost the title and had my winning streak ended. It hit home. I said something to the media but I was on autopilot. More words, as empty as I felt. Then I went back and cried my eyes out.

10

DYING TO WIN

I am dying on the floor in Sheffield. Another lung-busting, leg-sapping 800 metres is behind me. I feel empty. Chell stands over me and is talking away. Something snaps. I summon up some breath and shout: 'Do I look like I can bloody talk!'

Everybody has upped their game this year. Everybody is tense. We are pretending it is the same as any other season, but it isn't. The closer it gets, the more it affects me. TV adverts are playing with my face on. Andy pauses them and makes a joke. I cringe. This is my one opportunity. My one shot. It is scary.

As much as I felt honoured to be talked of as the 'Face of the Games' I didn't ask for or apply for the title. A journalist asks me what the process is of signing up for the title, as if it is something official. I found it a little uncomfortable as I don't have an ego and I say it was the media who decided it. I am bit embarrassed and feel there are any number of faces of the Games. However, I did not reject the tag and enjoyed a lot of the sponsor and media stuff I did, I wanted people to know my name, but it is pressure. More pressure. Rising all the time.

And so I snap. Sometimes I storm off and cry in the toilets at the EIS when I don't feel that the session has gone well. I don't let Chell see that and normally save it until I go home. Sometimes I go and sit in the car and stew. One day I start up the engine and drive to Leeds for my physio session with Ali. Chell knows he has overstepped the mark and keeps ringing, but I refuse to answer. That time he comes up to Leeds. I do not want to talk about it.

I know that he sometimes thinks I am whingeing. When we started out I trusted him because he was older and knew everything. But, as the years go by, your own knowledge gets deeper and you realize that this is a massive part of your life and you have to take some responsibility too. You're not a puppet. You can't rely wholly on other people any more. If things go wrong I need to know why. If we are doing a 200 metres session at this time of the year I need to know the reason. He finds the questioning hard, but I am not trying to be disrespectful. Nevertheless, he finds it offensive and some-times storms off himself and I am just left there on my own. Pressure rising. Sometimes I think, with injuries, he feels things are out of his control. He gets angry and says we will pull out of this or that. We both fly off the handle. It is a weird relationship. It's a business partnership but closer than that. And, beneath all the snapping and tears, the huffing and puffing, and beneath all that pressure, it works.

The build-up to London had started at the end of 2011. I had sat in a coffee shop across from the athletes' village in Daegu and pushed my silver medal around the Formica table. I said it was a medal to cherish but it wasn't what I'd wanted. Mo Farah had had another chance and got a gold in the 5,000 metres, but I had no opportunity to make amends. I'd keep the medal with all my others. They are in a box in my house. I don't have anything on display. I don't have photographs of me hanging on the walls. My mum keeps all the cuttings but I pile them in a corner of the office and maybe one day will get round to looking at them.

We normally do a five week block of training at the start of a new year and then Chell gives us a series of tests to do to gauge where we are against previous years. This time he gave us only three weeks. I was mad again.

'Why are you testing us so early?'

'I just want to get a baseline of where we are,' he said.

'But I don't want to test now. I haven't done enough.'

He got his way. There were around fourteen of us in the group for 2012. I saw Hannah, my friend and former training partner, and she said, jokingly, I deserved a medal just for putting up with Chell for so long.

'Say that again and I will squirt you in the face with this bottle,' I said after more harsh words.

He did and so I unleashed my bottle all over him and then ran off. He chased me but the training had obviously paid off because he could not catch me. There was always humour mixed with rage.

Sometimes it is hard at the EIS. It is a public space and so there are a lot of kids who come down to do their school sport. They get there at 9 a.m. and gradually it gets louder and louder. We usually booked the back straight and toiled away as privately as we could, but it was not easy. It was lovely to see the kids enjoying themselves, but sometimes it was difficult to strike the balance. Teachers would ask me to go over and say hello and, while I was happy to, sometimes I'd be asked to give a ten-minute speech when I should have been training. I found it hard to say no and occasionally the teachers would ask a bit much. Then I'd be in the middle of a nightmare long-jump session and I would hear the kids all shouting: 'JESS-I-CA, JESS-I-CA, JESS-I-CA!'

I figured that it was good practice for the Olympics, having people scrutinize you when things were going badly.

I had never trained as hard as I did that winter. Chell says he wrote out a training plan, with bells and whistles and a cherry on top, and then ripped it up. He called it the Olympic disease, the urge to try too hard. Instead, he said I should be training at between 96 and 100 per cent of my maximum effort in training. It did not have to be all flat out. The key then was to raise that lower band so that I was training at a higher level. Every year he wanted to move training on 5 per cent so I would run harder and faster and do three weights sessions instead of two, followed by 150 sit-ups and more over-distance running work.

The attention was becoming harder too. At one point in 2012 a woman came up to Sheffield purporting to be a journalist with *The Times*. Then she said she was from another newspaper. She began bugging my aunty and uncle and then pitched up on Dad's doorstep at 8 a.m. one day asking for an interview. Dad said I should talk to Jane and do it the proper way. The woman would not go away, though, and then ambushed my grandma and said she was writing an article about strong women. It was all a cover and she was just looking for some dirt. My family kept it from me until after the Olympics and I was glad because that would have really upset me and made me worried. This is my stuff and I don't want it affecting my family. Jane had warned me to expect it in Olympic year and I knew people would be sniffing around for a story. Although we had nothing to hide, no family is perfect.

In February things escalated when diver Tom Daley's coach accused him of doing too much media and promotional work. A few journalists tried to jump on the bandwagon and drag me into it. That really annoyed me because I had never missed training. I did work for my sponsors on my one day off. People who had no idea about me said I should be resting then, but I liked it and it was an outlet. These people also forget that we do not get paid ridiculous amounts of money like footballers, and we make most of our income through commercial deals. You get Lottery funding, which is means-tested, but I was not really getting paid to run until I'd become a world champion. There just isn't the appearance money on the way up. I realized then that people were after negative stuff and wanted to put a spin on the truth.

My first indoor competitions of the year were in Sheffield in January. I did the shot put at the Northern Championships, a modest loosener of 13.95 metres, and then did the long jump and 60 metres hurdles at the McCain Indoor City Challenge three weeks later, clocking 6.19 metres and 8.05 seconds respectively. The year was built around three dates. The first would be the World Indoor Championships in Istanbul in March, where I would be defending my title, the second was a return to Götzis in May and the third was Friday 3 August, the start of the Olympic heptathlon. That was journey's end.

The trials for the World Indoors were also on home

turf at the EIS in Sheffield in February. I twice matched my personal best of 7.95 seconds in the 60 metres hurdles and claimed the national titles for that event and the high jump, where I reached 1.91 metres. It was a good start. 'Promising,' I said in a press conference, but I knew that everybody was going to be in top shape for Olympic year. Being as good as before was not going to be enough. A week later, on 18 February, I went to the Aviva Grand Prix and clocked 7.87 seconds, a big personal best for the hurdles, the fastest time in the year and one that saw me take the scalp of Danielle Carruthers, the American specialist who had been runner-up in the solo event in Daegu. It put me in good spirits as I headed to Instanbul.

My grandad always rang me before major competitions. He had been there at the start, waiting impatiently at Don Valley as another coaching session with Chell overran by 45 minutes or so. My family and I have a reputation for always being early, so our contrasting approach to timekeeping was another testing area for me and Chell. Before Turkey Grandad rang me and gave me his advice.

'Relax,' was a regular mantra. 'Stay focused on your technique.'

'All right, Grandad.'

After Daegu, he rang and said: 'I've been having a think about your javelin.'

Everybody had. The press were talking of it as if it was

a huge problem and a major weakness. If I had matched my personal best then I would have actually won the world title by a single point, and I thought it was just a blip. Mick had felt terrible about it because it was the only event he was coaching, but it was not his fault. I never felt that way, but as soon as I got back he rang me up and said we needed to meet at the EIS, and he came along with reams of paper and notes about what we were going to work on. He was so frustrated, but I had just written it off as one of those things. Sometimes it just doesn't happen. There doesn't always have to be a major flaw. I had missed a lot of training and it had gone wrong. Simple as that. We made a slight change to my run-up because we had not been as consistent with it as normal in 2011 and we made a few minor tweaks to my technique.

There would be no javelin in Istanbul for the indoor pentathlon at the World Indoor Championships. The javelin and the 200 metres are the events that are not included in the five-event competition. I felt fantastic after my start to the year and knew I was running better than ever. It was so refreshing to go into a championship with a clean block of training and no injury scares.

I went to the pre-event press conference with Mo, Charles van Commenee and Tiffany Porter, who had been made the team captain. I had been asked but said I would rather not, because I just did not feel I wanted any extra distractions as I prepared for London. They asked Tiffany and, at the press conference, a journalist asked her to recite the National Anthem. It was really uncomfortable. I think naming Tiffany as the captain put her in an awkward situation because it opened her up to be questioned about the whole 'plastic Brit' thing. It was hard on her.

Everyone was aware of the talk in the media, but there was no divide in the team. I was directly affected by it because I really wanted the British hurdles record and Tiffany came in and took it straightaway. I was frustrated but she had a passport and it was all legit. It was not something I could control so I did not worry about it. Tiffany is a really nice girl and I thought it must have been hard coming into an established team and trying to be part of that, so I tried to be as welcoming as possible.

The arena was on the outskirts of Istanbul, away from the hustle and bustle of the chaotic centre and the boats bobbing up and down the Bosporus. I saw the other girls and there were some nods and hellos. For Dobrynska it was going to be a particularly tough event because her husband – who was also her coach – was at home in the Ukraine where he was seriously ill with cancer. Chernova, meanwhile, was the world champion and had already scythed a huge amount off her best time in the hurdles in the build-up.

I was in lane five for the hurdles with Dobrynska

outside me. The indoor event is so quick that there is no margin for error. A mistake and you are done for. The gun sounded and 7.91 seconds later I had won the race. Chernova and Dobrynska were second and third.

The pentathlon takes place on one day, instead of two, so there was not long to wait until the high jump. I jump from the left side off my right foot with most of the girls jumping off their left foot from the right side. That meant that I was in the minority when I turned up to the high-jump area and saw a bright yellow contraption close to where I would take off. It was distracting. Chell had clocked it and was shouting down to me from the stands to get it moved. I asked an official, but he said they couldn't do anything. It was in line with the finish of the sprint straight and held the beam that measured times.

There was nothing I could do so I just got on with it. I sailed over the first few heights but hit problems at 1.87 metres. I got over that at the last attempt, but could not manage 1.90 metres, which was frustrating given that I had already jumped it that season.

My shot put was good. I finished with 14.79 metres, a personal best that suggested Chell might have been right when he said I could top 15 metres, but Dobrynska led the way with a huge 16.51 metres. It meant that, after three out of five events, I led Lithuania's Austra Skujyte by just 10 points with Dobrynska another 19 adrift.

Coming home – in the airport in South Korea with Chell, Mum, Carmel and Dad. The old man found the family conversation very stimulating!

Just an ordinary girl – with Andy and my parents as I get my MBE in 2011.

Indoor fireworks – the World Indoor title defence starts well in Istanbul in 2012.

But then falls apart in the long jump.

Ouch – my physio Ali Rose with her metal thumbs.

Raising the bar in Götzis.

Team Ennis Part 1 – Bricey, Derry, Ali and Chell.

Team Ennis Part 2 — Jane and Suzi help me celebrate my win in Götzis.

Let the Games begin — Mum and Dad before heading to the Olympic Opening Ceremony in London.

Above: 'I'm not having that' — the crowd lift me and I overtake in the last 100m of the 800m.

Right: Generation gap — flying in the 200m with Katarina Johnson-Thompson outside me.

Below: Chell gives me coaching advice — rocking those shades.

Above: Heading out for the high jump — the stadium was full and the atmosphere was incredible.

Left: Journey's end — I am the Olympic champion.

Above right: Sebastian Coe had promised to present me with my gold medal — and so he did.

Right: A family affair — with my parents and Carmel at Team GB house on the night I became the champion.

18 May 2013: A wonderful new chapter in my life – Mrs Ennis-Hill

And then I crumbled in the long jump. My best was a mere 6.19 metres, while Dobrynska did a season's best of 6.57 metres. Suddenly Dobrynska was 93 points ahead of me. Skujyte was up to second. If I had felt invincible a year ago, I didn't now.

It left me with another 800 metres where I knew I had to run incredibly to win. I needed to put six seconds on Dobrynska. I gave it everything and won the race. As I came over the line I saw the scoreboard flash up my name and points tally of 4965. The letters 'CR' indicating a championship record were next to it. I broke out into a smile. I'd won! I did not see Chell in the crowd at that point, shouting, 'No, no, no.' In the emotional aftermath of the competition, mentally and physically drained, it did not occur to me that the indoor track was small and Dobrynska had not been that far behind. Then her name flashed up ahead of mine. The score of 5013 points was a world record. It suddenly clicked that they were amending the scores with each name flashed up. So it was silver again, and this time it was even worse than Daegu. To have been lifted so high and then dropped so quickly was awful. The emotions were intensified. It was a horrible moment.

I did not begrudge Dobrynska. To win with a world record was truly special. I also knew what a tough time she was having with her husband so ill. She's a nice woman and I congratulated her, but I felt horrible. It was tough to sit in doping, with her behind me in the queue, red-eyed and fighting my emotions.

Andy dragged me out for a drink that night. Then I got an abrupt message from Chell to get back to the hotel because I needed treatment. I was not feeling great and would have preferred just to have some time away with Andy, but I went back in a taxi. Andy did his best to comfort me.

'You are a consistent winner of medals,' he told me on that journey through the crowded streets. 'If you have a bad day it's a silver medal. That's not a bad place to be.'

It actually cheered me up. The whole thing of thinking I'd won and having it taken away from me hurt like hell, but Andy had a way of saying the right things.

I had lost two world titles in little more than six months. Dobrynska now looked to be the Olympic favourite and clearly had a knack of getting herself into the perfect shape for competition. Chernova had had a bad time at the World Indoors but I expected her to be back too. There were others who might sneak into the equation too. It was getting harder by the day. In Daegu my javelin had let me down. In Istanbul my long jump had. I needed to sort them both out or I was going to get nothing in London.

It is easy to get paranoid as an athlete, and the nearer you get to competitions, the worse that can get. We are always told to be ultra-careful about our health. In the build-up to the Olympics the message was 'germs cost medals'. Nobody was shaking hands in case they picked up something. Everyone was using anti-bacterial sprays. It may sound obsessive, but the Olympics are an obsession.

It meant I was not best pleased when Andy's brother, Matt, knocked on the door one day close to the Games. I went to give him a kiss and he backed away.

'Don't come near me,' he said. 'I'm full of cold.'

I was a bit incredulous. 'Matt, why did you come here, then?'

We went out for a meal but I stayed down the other end of the table. Afterwards I was quite stroppy and did ask Andy why Matt had visited if he was ill. And then I did get a cold and Matt posted a message from a safe distance on Facebook saying that he hoped he had not ruined Jessica's Olympic dream. He'd meant no harm, but Olympic planning is all about the small details.

I was stewing even more at my next race. It was May, and I was back at the Great City Games, where I was running 100 metres hurdles in Manchester city centre. It was a true test for me because I was up against Dawn Harper, the reigning Olympic champion at the event, and Danielle Carruthers, the runner-up at the World Championships in Daegu.

I had been suffering a bit with a cold but I ran well.

It was one of those days when it felt effortless. I beat them all to the line and the time, a new best of 12.75 seconds, flashed up. I was ecstatic. But again, just like in Istanbul, it was short-lived. It was my old rival, Kelly Sotherton, watching on television, who alerted people to the fact something was awry.

'Thought 100m hurdles was great but I'm sure there were only nine hurdles not ten,' she tweeted. She was right. The organizers had only put out nine hurdles and so any times and records did not count in the official stats. It was a silly mistake and an unbelievable one. I was genuinely angry afterwards and let my frustration show in the interviews I gave afterwards. 'I feel let down,' I said. 'It felt like it was a good race, I was running well, I was obviously coming through at the end, stick another hurdle on there and it would have been the same outcome but, argh, I'm so annoyed.'

People wondered how we had not realized we were a hurdle short, but you don't count when you are running. I thought it seemed a long run to the end, but you are so in the moment that you do not see the bigger picture. 'I can't believe that,' I continued. 'It's a great event but that's a massive, massive mess-up. As an athlete you expect that everything should be set up properly and there should be no mistakes like that.'

Kelly, who was still hoping to make the team in London in the heptathlon, tweeted again when she realized it was becoming a story. 'I feel bad! People probably think I'm being a cow bag!'

The organizers, Nova International, issued an apology. I understood people get things wrong, but it was a pretty basic mistake and I wanted everything to be right this year. Already I had lost in Istanbul and I needed things to start clicking into place.

Chell said he had never seen me like that before. I don't like conflict but it got to me. I think the pressure of the whole year got to me. I was upset and mad. Andy drove me home and I rang my mum to talk it through. I was already getting tetchy and tense ahead of Götzis the following week and Andy was already walking on eggshells around me, but I hadn't gone to Manchester to have fun. It's never ever just fun for me. Even a throwing event in Barnsley is deadly serious. Chell rang and was adamant he needed to speak to me, but I didn't have time for him. He couldn't understand why I was so annoyed. The next day Andy Caine, from the organizers, rang me up. He apologized but by that time I had softened and said: 'Oh, it's fine, just one of those things.' They sent flowers too. I love the event and have never slagged it off, but it was an almighty cock-up. I just wanted things to go smoothly for once. So we flew out a few days later to the Hypo-Meeting in Götzis for what was a huge meeting, the final heptathlon before the Olympics, and that was when Fatgate broke and things got even stranger.

11

TRIALS & TRIBULATIONS

The headline in the *Guardian* read:

> *Jessica Ennis coach hits out at UK Athletics for labelling her 'fat'.*

It was Friday 25 May, the day before the heptathlon started in Götzis. The gist of the story was that Chell reportedly said a 'high-ranking coach' within our sport – he refused to say who – had suggested 'that she's out of condition and she's got too much weight'.

It quickly became a big story about me being accused of being fat, with lots of people wading in and saying how ridiculous it was. Eating disorder groups were rung up and said this sort of story did not help their cause. And, of course, the media wanted to know who it was who had said the words in question.

It was irritating because it was another distraction. Olympic year threw up lots of different challenges and, in any other year, issues like this would not have gained anything like the same attention. Chell had been annoyed that the person in question had suggested I might be carrying too much weight as he is very sensitive about the impact of discussing weight issues with athletes, particularly female athletes. Neither of us expected the story to be printed on the eve of competition. Suddenly 'Fatgate', as some dubbed it, was big news.

I was not bothered about the stories personally. I was happy with how I was performing and was happy with my body so I felt secure in myself. I let it wash over me – I didn't want to make the story any bigger. However, it did make me think about the messages that the story was sending out to kids. They probably looked at me and thought I was really skinny, so to hear that people might regard me as fat could create issues, not for me but for other people. That did bother me because it is important.

The words and meaning ended up twisted, but once it came out I knew what it was referring to. As an athlete you look at your body in a very different way to a 'normal person'. It's all about muscle and fat ratio, so I think the remarks were more in that athletic context. It was not a general 'you're fat' remark. But it did go out of control for a few days and I do think you have to be careful and sensitive when talking about people's weight, in whatever context it might be. If I had not been performing well then that would have knocked me and maybe I would have thought, 'Yeah, maybe I am a bit heavy'. That would have got me really down, but I was in a happy state at the time of Götzis.

Chell was being defensive but there was no need. Götzis showed that. It was one event that went like a dream. I was fast in the hurdles, average in the high jump and then everything just clicked. It was seamless, the 14.51 metres in the shot put connected to a 22.88 personal best in the 200 metres. It was a delicious domino effect and, by the time I had equalled my personal best of 6.51 metres in the long jump, I was 251 points clear of Chernova and 415 ahead of Dobrynska. The latter's poor form was understandable. In the interim between Istanbul and Götzis, Dobrynska's husband had lost his battle against cancer. It put things in perspective and made me realize just how astonishing her performance had been in Turkey. While the stories about my weight were raging on that sunny Friday morning, I went over to her and said how sorry I was. Sometimes, in the blinkered world of sport, it is easy to lose sight of the truly weighty matters.

I was on a high, though, as I threw the javelin 47.11 metres, a personal best and a pointed message to all those people who had suggested I couldn't throw after Daegu. I realized that finally Denise Lewis's record was there for the taking. I also did the calculations with Chell and knew that a time of 2 minutes 9 seconds in the 800 metres would break the 6900 points barrier, something only seven women had ever done.

I ran the 800 metres perfectly in terms of the time. I won the competition and added 75 points to Denise's record. Yet Chernova had done everything in her power to pass me in the last few yards of the last event, our final duel before London. It did not affect the scores, but it obviously gave her some confidence. As I spoke to reporters on the infield she was doing the same. 'It was a great personal best,' Chernova said of my efforts. 'But in the next competition it will be, "Can she beat that record? Can she get the same points or not?" I know what I can do and I will work towards that. I'm not afraid of anything. If people just look at one girl, it will be very hard for her to compete. I'm very popular in my country and my country is bigger than Great Britain.'

I didn't care what she said. There were two months to go and, whatever anyone might have thought, I was in the shape of my life.

As a multi-eventer it is not often that you get invited to Diamond League events, the big, glamour nights where the best athletes in the world get to compete. I had run in New York before, but the chance to hurdle at the world-famous Bislett Stadium in Oslo in June was perfect for me.

I love hurdling. I always have done. And in Oslo I would be up against Sally Pearson, the Australian who had taken the event by storm. She looked odds-on to upgrade her silver medal from Beijing and was the reigning world champion, indoors and out. Also in the field were the likes of Tiffany Porter and Lolo Jones. I felt confident. Not for one moment did I think I would beat Sally, but I felt I could beat my lifetime best. Then, with the sun bathing the famous old stadium in evening light, and Usain Bolt limbering up for his 100 metres, I jumped the gun. I stood impassively in my lane, trying to disbelieve the reality, but was then shown a red card. I was disqualified. Now I knew how stupid Bolt must have felt the year before at the World Championships. I walked back under the stand and felt crushed. I had wanted to show that multi-eventers are not merely average at everything. I wanted to show I could compete against the best. But instead I had blown it and it was another thing in the back of my head going into the Olympics, another seed of doubt planted.

I had got all my media and sponsor commitments out of the way beforehand. There had been talk in the media about how much I was now earning. Some of the figures were way off, but I was making a good living now and had forged long-term relationships with a number of companies – Adidas, Jaguar, Olay, Powerade, BP, British Airways, Aviva and Omega. The bigger profile helped enormously in some ways.

That was certainly the case with my shoes. My first spikes had been the hand-me-down shoes from Chell's ex-wife, Nicola. At the time I felt special to have spikes rather than my normal trainers, but as you get more serious you need different shoes for different events. The shot-put shoes are smoother to match the surface of the circle, the high-jump ones have more grip on the heel and the hurdles ones are lighter and put you on your toes. After winning the world title, I was at a level where Adidas would talk to me about my specific requirements. Mark Dannhauser from the athletes' services department came over from Germany to watch me train and talk to me about the shoes they were making. In 2011 they had a long-jump shoe that had a zip on them. I said I didn't think the zip was needed and just created more bulk, so they got rid of it and went with laces. It was great to have that input and I think they valued my opinion; obviously because I am a heptathlete, I have to wear more shoes than most.

As London approached, the demands from the sponsors and media grew. It was another time that I felt I had to be firm. Sponsors wanted me to go down to the Olympic Stadium for shoots, but I refused all of them. The reason was I wanted it to be new and fresh when I got there. I wanted that adrenaline buzz. I wanted to see the stadium when it was full of people rather than an empty arena. I had been there once, when it was still a building site and there was no track down, but the next time I went there I wanted to get that rush of newness.

There were other offers too that I felt strongly about.

A local BBC film crew wanted to follow me up to the Olympics. I didn't want to do it. Chell was keen and said it was not about me, it was about him. I got annoyed. I didn't mean it arrogantly, but I said: 'It's not about you, is it? It's me running that they will be filming.' I was strongly against the idea, but Chell let the guy come. I had nothing against the people involved – they were lovely – but it was not something I needed. One day Chell asked if they could go and film an interview with my mum and dad. I didn't want that either. My mum has done a few things, but they are private people and don't like being in the spotlight.

'Why don't they go and film your mum if it's all about you?' I asked him. He shrugged and walked off.

As London got nearer, though, Chell and I were communicating well. We were in this together, thirteen years of joy and pain coming down to these two days in Stratford. Sometimes Chell would be concerned I was doing too much and would tell me to take an afternoon off. I would refuse that too. If I missed an afternoon for anything then I would wonder where we were going to make it up.

There were two weeks between Oslo and the Olympic trials which doubled as the UK Championships. I threw the javelin and did the long jump in Bedford in the interim and then went to the Alexander Stadium in Birmingham for the trials, which were being held from

Friday 12 July to Sunday 14 July. Unlike many competing that weekend, my place in the team had already been decided. I also knew that Louise Hazel and Katarina Johnson-Thompson would be my heptathlon team-mates. Kat was only nineteen and had produced a string of personal bests to get the qualifying standard while I was in Oslo. She is certainly the star of the future and has already beaten my junior records. I was pleased for her.

However, the trials were still important for me and the first day was mixed. I won the hurdles but struggled in the high jump. The warm-up for the latter was seriously shocking and I failed to clear any height. I was panicking a bit and went over to Chell.

'What's wrong? What's wrong?'

I could see in his face that he was worried. He looked a bit lost. He will hate me for saying this, but he told me I could pull out, that I didn't need to go through with it. I am not sure why he said it. I don't know if he was worried I'd embarrass myself or if he didn't want me to get beaten so close to the Olympics. Maybe it was reverse psychology or just a desire for me not to worry about having a poor jump next to my name. But I said I couldn't pull out. If things went badly at the Olympics I'd have to deal with that. It would be a bad habit to get into and I'm not a quitter. The competition started and I cleared every height up to 1.89 metres at the first attempt. I took the UK title and mocked Chell.

'Pull out, eh? Didn't have faith, did you?'

But the warm-up and the inconsistency had been unnerving. I couldn't put my finger on it, but reasoned that I should go back to basics. Sometimes you don't run the curve well and forget to lean away from the bar. So I thought, 'Don't overcomplicate it, run a good curve and lean.' That's what had given me my personal best of 1.95 metres back in 2007.

The next day was worse. The long jump was still a problem. At Bedford I had done four fouls before getting in one decent jump of 6.40 metres. The grey clouds in Birmingham hovered over me as I started the competition in front of the main stand. It became an exercise in frustration. I lost my rhythm on the runway and then found myself having to speed up on the board. Then I was over the board. My position was all wrong and so I was fouling or pulling out of jumps and running through the pit with a look of deepening exasperation. In total, it meant that from my last twelve jumps in two competitions I had done seven fouls and two run-throughs. It was scarcely ideal preparation for London, but time was running out. My brain was wrecking.

When things go wrong I want to see Chell straightaway. I want to repair the damage instantly. He was upbeat, saying we could put it right, but I knew we were running out of time. It was one month until the start of the Olympics and I was in tatters.

12

COUNTDOWN

I am on the balcony of our hotel room at Club Quinta da Ria. It is another beautiful day, light blue skies reflected in the pool. It would be an idyllic scene but for the black mood festering away. I have just had the worst long-jump session I could have imagined. Every effort was a no-jump. There is a fortnight to go. Nicola Sanders, my room-mate, is in when I get back and so I move out to the balcony. I ring Andy and pour out my heart and fears. I can't do it. I'm going to mess it all up in the long jump. What if all this work is for nothing?

The saving grace was that before going to the Team GB holding camp in Monte Gordo, Portugal, I had done some good sessions with Chell and Bricey.

'Don't worry, we can sort this out,' Bricey said. We filmed every jump and then analysed it in slow-mo. Bricey went away to crunch the numbers, returning to tell me how much vertical lift I was getting. Then we decided to take the run-up back a bit. We had to try everything after the disaster in Birmingham.

I had stopped reading the newspapers or watching the news. I did not trawl the Internet or spend much time on Twitter. You really do not want to be reading something bad on there so close to the Games. I was in lockdown. I didn't want to talk about the Olympics. Before flying to Portugal I held a baby shower for my friend Charlotte at my house. It was good to see friends and catch up with normal life. I rarely like to go on about the Olympics. If anything, my friend Katie is the one who gets a bit excited and says how wonderful and amazing my achievements are, and complains that I don't tell her everything. But that's Katie and I love her to bits for it. I said my goodbyes to my friends and family and flew to Portugal. It would be three weeks until I saw Andy again, by which time it would all be over. As ever, Grandad told me to relax and and stay focused on my technique.

There was a relaxed atmosphere in Portugal and I liked sharing with Nicola. We usually talked more about *Grey's Anatomy* than the Olympics. We often watched it on our laptops. Earlier on in the year I had thought we were at the same stage and so mentioned a main character dying.

'What!' she cried.

'Oh, er, well, he might not have.'

A day later she saw him coughing up blood and so I was well and truly rumbled. The look she gave me could have killed.

Most things were going well. I had some great hurdles sessions and felt confident in that. Hurdling can be scary. The key for me is in bringing your lead leg down before you have actually cleared the hurdle with your trailing leg, thereby reducing your time over the hurdles. That is quite a daunting thing to do because your instinct wants you to clear it comfortably. Get it a fraction out and you will clatter a hurdle and there is a fine line between a fast time and falling. I remembered back to the last Olympics when Lolo Jones, the American, had the gold medal in the bag in the 100 metres hurdles. She was clear and almost home. Almost. Six letters but a huge word. She hit the penultimate hurdle and dropped way back. Her one shot was a blank. I knew my lead leg was a bit straight. It always had been but the sessions were good and I was confident. The same went for the 800 metres. I had a good time-trial in the scorching heat on the Algarve and knew that boded well for the cooler climes of London. Everything was going well. Everything except the cursed long jump.

I was glad that we were in Portugal. I could imagine how mad everything was going at home and was happy that UKA had decided long ago that we would be basing ourselves out here in relative anonymity, rather than in

Aldershot, which had been the original plan and where it would have been far harder to shield us from the hype.

There had been talk about getting the likes of Cathy Freeman and Michael Johnson, the Australian and American Olympic legends, to talk to us about the pressure of a home Games. I was not too bothered. I respected their achievements, but felt I was on my own path. And, anyway, I was looking forward to a big crowd.

On the night of the Opening Ceremony, the team gathered in the hotel's auditorium. It felt like an age since there had been a public debate about how the athletes were being denied the chance to go to the ceremony. I certainly didn't feel that way. The ceremonies and countdowns were more for the public. The athletes were going to the Olympics to do a job.

We wore the same garish gold and white tracksuits worn by those athletes who did make the ceremony. We had the BBC on and the presenter said it would only be another forty minutes before Team GB came in, but the athletes' parade seemed to drag on forever. My parents had gone to the ceremony and Mum texted me. 'There are a lot of people here,' she said. That made me laugh. She later said that she was worried because of the noise and thought of me being in front of 80,000 people, but I thrive on pressure and didn't think that was going to be a problem. Then Jessica Zelinka, one of the other heptathletes who had arrived in London, sent me a message. 'It's like a Jessica Ennis theme park,' she tweeted. I laughed at that, but did begin to think, 'Oh my God.'

We had the team speeches while we were in Portugal. Charles van Commenee liked to make jokes, but sometimes they got lost. The theme of his speech was journeys. He looked at Greg Rutherford, the long jumper, and called him 'the man of glass' because he said he was always injured. Little did we know what he'd go on to achieve. Then he mentioned many other athletes with positive and slightly negative statements. By the time he labelled Nigel Levine 'the Joker', Nicola got the giggles and I had to look down and try to stop going the same way. Nobody else was making a sound. Charles continued, talking of the challenges he faced, even mentioning 'Fatgate', but then got interrupted. A mainstay of his speeches was some light-hearted banter directed at the hard-to-decipher Scandinavian accent of Aki Salo, who worked with the relay team. This time Fuzz Ahmed, the RADA-trained coach of high jumper Robbie Grabarz, hijacked the speech and a video of Aki came up on the screen. However, the perfectly clipped vowels of Lawrence Clarke, an Old Etonian hurdler and heir apparent to a baronetcy, had been dubbed over Aki's words. That brought the house down.

The 400 metres hurdles world champion, Dai Greene was expected to do very well in London. His captain's speech was more natural than mine and included a sly dig at me because I kept saying to him, 'how's your speech going,' and winding him up – his praise of the juniors in the team including the suggestion that Kat could give me some long-jump lessons. There was a good atmosphere that night, but the reality was now dawning on us. The Olympics, the goal that had always seemed so far away, was here. This was our time. Would I capture the moment or let it slip?

I had never competed in London before, not even at Crystal Palace, the UK's biggest track meet. It was a new experience for me. I was just glad that we had flown to City Airport and not Heathrow, where BA had painted my face over an area the size of fifteen tennis courts in a field. This was a welcome for arriving athletes and was used to boast on Twitter about the menace of #homeadvantage. I had thought it was on private land when I was told about the idea, but then I found out it was just a field. I expected a bunch of kids to go out there armed with spray cans and spades. Things had certainly taken a turn for the weird.

The Olympic Village was an assault on the senses. From the calm and quiet of Portugal, we were plunged into this swirling mass of noise and colour. From the enormous dining hall to the armed police, it was daunting and overwhelming. We went to check our rooms. They were basic but fine, and I was sharing an apartment with a great bunch – Nicola, Goldie Sayers, Lee McConnell, Yammy Aldama, Kate Dennison and Eilidh Child.

Sometimes it is easy to stay in your bubble and forget what everyone else is going through, but I felt so sorry for Goldie, one of the nicest people you could wish to meet. She had been in great form and had broken the British record at Crystal Palace before flying out to the training camp. However, she had also suffered a serious injury in London. She said she could throw but then the pain was excruciating. She had to give it a go, but she was a victim of the worst possible timing. I was gutted for her.

Phillips Idowu was another who was struggling with injury. He had been the world champion in the triple jump in 2009 and had a habit of producing his best on the biggest stage. However, he had decided to stay in London and receive treatment there rather than fly out to Portugal. It became a story, fuelled by the fact he did not see eye to eye with Charles. In London people began to speculate whether he would turn up or not. Charles even called him 'the invisible man', but I just thought it was really sad because he obviously had an injury and was trying to deal with it the best way he could. Like Goldie, it would be awful for him that he just did not have enough time to get it right.

For the main part, though, I was taking in the new surroundings. We had barely dumped our bags when Nicola spied Prince William and Kate Middleton coming into the village. We dropped our bags, ran down the stairs and strategically positioned ourselves where they could not miss us.

'Oh, hi Jess,' said William.

I thought, this is getting weirder still. Then Kate asked us about the village before Prince Harry piped up.

'Not much pressure on you, then.'

The dining hall was so big that you would always look for someone else to go with. It was like being back at school again, a scrawny child standing with a tray in the canteen trying to find a friendly face to sit with. The rooms were basic but good, somewhere, I imagine, between prison and halls of residence, but I would hardly be there because I was always one of the first to leave and last back. Usually, I am quite conscientious and tiptoe around if I am sharing. This time I was glad to have my own room. The only thing that was disconcerting was when I had a quick look on Twitter and a found a twenty-year-old boy, who was on the cleaning staff, had declared excitably that he had just been in Jessica Ennis's room. That freaked me out a bit.

The next day I visited the stadium. I wanted to know where the combined events room was and the route from the warm-up track into the stadium. Then it was up to the Main Press Centre, a huge building on the edge of the Olympic Park where the world's media were based, and I joined Dai, Greg Rutherford, and Charles at the Team GB press conference.

The park was packed. People were dressed in Union Jack outfits and the purple-vested volunteers were merrily helping everyone on their way. I went back to the apartment and watched some of the other events. It was Wednesday 1 August. I tried to put the long jump out of my mind and clung to the fact that I had managed to have one better session before I left Portugal. It was still there, though, in the back of my mind.

The next day was 2 August, the eve of competition. I did my usual routine, withdrew into myself a bit and went over everything with Chell. My mum sent me her usual text.

'Don't let those big girls push you around.'

It was sixteen years since I had turned up to the Don Valley Stadium because my mum was a firm believer in tiring out kids, four years since I had been in the deepest depression over Beijing, but I did not allow myself to get emotional. I went over every event six times in my head, how I wanted them to pan out. From my balcony I could see the Olympic Stadium, lit up and softening the darkness. Tomorrow morning I would be there for the hurdles. I lay in bed and pictured perfect technique. My mind wandered and I fell, so I tried again. When I had cleared all the obstacles a few times I drifted off to sleep.

13

EIGHTY
THOUSAND
FRIENDS

The alarm clock rang at 5.50 a.m. I got up and went to the dining hall. Even at that time there were a lot of people there. I had some Granola cereal, coffee and some juice. Most of Team Ennis were there too. I could sense the nerves. Doc went and got a cinnamon swirl. As he came back, Derry said: 'Oh, I think I'll have one too.' So Doc went back for another. As he came back with it, someone else piped up and asked Doc to get them one. It was silly but I laughed. It was a temporary release from the stranglehold of tension.

We took the bus down to the warm-up track. There were tents around it for each team. I lay on the physio's couch and listened to some music on my iPod. Normally, I am twitchy and feel a mounting sense of anxiety, but this time I felt a strange calmness flowing over me. I thought, 'That's weird.'

To get to the stadium from the warm-up track you had to walk through a long tented tunnel. The eight women in my hurdles heat were led along it one by one. Two places in front of me was Chernova, tall and thin and ready. We emerged from the tunnel in the bowels of the stadium and went into the call room. Our bags and spikes were checked. There was a TV on in the room showing the other heats. Kat was in the one before mine. I saw her on the TV and her face widened with a huge grin when her name was read out. I noticed for the first time that there seemed to be a lot of people in the stadium.

Then it was our turn. They called us up and we walked out through a tunnel and up into the light. For the first time I realized how big and frightening the Olympics are. I glanced around and was amazed that the stadium was full. Even though I knew they had sold the tickets, I'd never been to a championship where the morning session was heaving with people and expectation like this. By now I was really nervous.

We lined up. I am always very deadpan on the line before the hurdles because this is where it can all start to go wrong. I did not even hear them call my name, I didn't know when to wave, but I sensed it. The adrenaline was huge but the crowd gave me confidence. One shot. Suddenly, all the nerves dropped and, then, I was ready to go.

I didn't think negative things. Dos not don'ts. I was in lane eight with Hyleas Fountain outside me in nine. That was good because she was a fine hurdler, but Jessica Zelinka, another strong athlete in the event, was over the other side of the track on the inside. I had been annoyed by that because she is a 12.68 runner and you want to be close to the fast girls. We crouched and the roar dropped to total silence. It was that special moment of bated breath and possibility. Then the gun went. I did not get out particularly well, but the pick-up was good and it flowed. It was a blur but I crossed the line and that was when I heard the crowd again; before it had been as if everything was suspended. I did not know if I had won because I could not see Jessica Zelinka. I clocked the time on the scoreboard as I went past, but I was not about to celebrate prematurely. I had done that in Istanbul and was not going to make the same mistake. Then the time and my name did come up on the board, high above the flaming cauldron.

12.54 seconds

I could not believe it. I put both hands in the air. It was a British record and the fastest anyone had ever done in a heptathlon. Later someone would tell me that the time would have given me the gold medal in the hurdles at the 2008 Olympics. It was beyond my expectations and I was numb.

It meant that after one event I was in the lead, with Zelinka second, Hyleas Fountain third and Chernova and Dobrynska fifteenth and twenty-second respectively. That could all change, of course. There are so many ways for fate to turn against you in the heptathlon, but I was off to a wonderful start.

There was very little time between the hurdles and the high jump. I could not afford to remain on that bouncy high and so I composed myself. I'd achieved one thing, now for the next task. It was the same in the Olympic Stadium as it had been in nursery, tearing from one activity to the next, never satisfied, always craving more.

Normally, we take everything with us when we leave the combined events room for the hurdles. This time the officials told us that they would bring all our gear out to us for the high jump. However, when we got to the high-jump area, there was no kit for any of the girls in that last hurdles heat. That caused a problem because the warm-up clock was already ticking down. We watched in frustration as girls from other hurdles heats took jump after jump, while we hung around awaiting the arrival of our stuff. Tempers flared because half of us had no jumping spikes and we could not mark out our run-ups. I went up to an official.

'Where are our bags?'

'They're coming,' one said.

It was way beyond a joke. It was getting close to the

start time for the high jump and there was a bunch of unsettled athletes. Hyleas was particularly annoyed. A few of us decided it would be quicker if we went back to the combined events room and got the bags ourselves, so we trotted off only to be told they were now on their way and someone was walking them out, around the entire perimeter of the track.

Hyleas had had enough. She decided it was time to protest, so a few girls went and sat on the high-jump mat to prevent the other girls from taking their practices. It was not what anyone needed in an Olympic final, but there was a sense of injustice out there in the morning sun. Finally, the bags arrived and the officials extended the warm-up time, but not before we'd been through an emotional wringer.

We stepped out our marks a start mark and a brake mark – and put tape down on the track. I am always careful about mine. Sometimes girls run over them and they get ripped up, but I've never seen anyone deliberately remove someone else's. My high jump was nowhere near where it was at its peak. After Daegu, Kat's coach, Mike Holmes – a top British high jump coach who had worked with former British number one Steve Smith – had done a session with us. He watched the video of me, turned to Chell and said: 'At least she put her number on the right way round.' I was terrified of him and he had a way of dragging me down to earth. I'd do a session, look at him and he would just shake his head and say, 'No.' I had tried hard to get back to my 2007 level, but I had lower expectations now. In London the weather turned on me too. There was a huge downpour in the middle of the event and, even though I knew the spikes would keep me safe, it inevitably made me a bit more tentative running the curve. I had one failure at 1.80 metres but got over 1.83 metres at the first attempt. By that stage Chernova had fallen by the wayside, bombing out at 1.80 metres. I don't do sums in my head and I don't know everyone's PBs, but I knew Chernova was off her world title pace. I needed another clearance though. Anything less than 1.86 metres would be a disaster, in my reckoning. I failed on the first two attempts. The crowd groaned as one. Dobrynska bowed out at 1.83 metres. It was a chance. My last chance. I thought about all the times I had pulled it out on the final attempt. 'This is what makes a champion,' I told myself.

The track had dried out quickly and I attacked. Run the curve and lean. I remember that moment when you stop climbing, just before you fall, that lovely plateau. Then I remember hitting the mat and I bounced up. The bar had stayed put. I smiled my relief. I was up in my hurdles and average in my high jump so I was in a good place. I left the track after two events and was collared by Phil Jones from the BBC. 'Speechless,' I told him when he asked me about the hurdles, but I found a few words anyway. 'I cannot believe I ran that time.' And the high jump? 'I am disappointed I did not get an extra height, but it's roughly where I was in Götzis.'

The shot put was in the evening session and so I went back to the combined events room. Most of the girls went back to the village, but Kat and I stayed. She was up to third place and was loving every minute of it. For me it was harder. Kat was going to enjoy the experience, knowing that her time was probably going to be in Rio in another four years, but for me this was it. This was my time. We were at different ends of the scale.

I was in a good lead and, significantly, Dobrynska was only twelfth and Chernova sixteenth. I was 218 points ahead of Chernova, although I knew she could get that back in the javelin and long jump. I was not thinking that far ahead, though. All that bothered me now was the shot put. The time passed slowly. One group of 80,000 people left the stadium after the morning session and another 80,000 packed in for the evening. Such a mass of humanity. I did not ring anyone in those interim hours. It was about recovering and preparing for the next task.

On the warm-up track New Zealand's champion shot putter Valerie Adams was practising next to me. She is a huge woman and immensely powerful. She said hello and then started doing amazing overhead throws. I suddenly felt very small again, my red, white and blue kit replaced by the red swimming costume of a nervous schoolgirl, and I felt her watching my technique. But I was confident in the shot. I had improved hugely and shown that size is not everything. Valerie would actually end up with a silver medal from London, but would finally get the gold weeks after her final because the winner, Belorussia's Nadzeya Ostapchuk, failed a dope test. Her coach claimed he had spiked her food with steroids and so she escaped with a one-year ban, but how sad that Valerie would not get to hear her anthem in the stadium.

My own shot was solid. I opened with 13.85 metres and improved it to 14.28 metres on my second attempt. The third was the worst of the lot. In my head, anything over 14 metres is not a calamity, although I had been throwing so well in Portugal that I half expected to get close to 15 metres, but it was good enough and I could not fail to notice how the others were struggling. Dobrynska almost had a disaster with two fouls before saving her Olympic defence with a final effort of 15.05 metres, while Chernova threw 14.17 metres, only equalling her mark from the World Championships. I felt confident as I headed into the 200 metres, the final event of the first day.

This was where all the toil was meant to pay off. Training was meant to be harder. That's what Chell said. That's why we did all those 300 metre reps in training. We did it so that, in those last 50 metres, when you are dying, you can hold it together.

'Technique,' Chell would shout on those endless days

in the Don Valley. 'Think about your running style.' Most of the time I didn't care about my running style because I just wanted to cross that line, but I had been forced to think about it because it's in those last yards when things fall apart.

Again I was in the last heat. Chernova was there too, along with Holland's Dafne Schippers, a real speed merchant who had clocked 22.69 seconds at the World Championships and who would be running in the individual 200 metres in London.

I am always nervous before the 200 metres because it feels such a long way. Beforehand we had been in the combined events room. Kat was smiling and thrilled. 'I can't wait,' she said. 'I'm so excited.' She was on her phone playing games in between the sessions, loving every minute and rightly so. Once again I reflected that for me, this was it.

I knew from the hurdles that the track was fast. The temperature had dropped and there was some wind swirling around, but it was a good race. Dafne was in the inside lane and I was in the outside one. I thought we could have a great battle. It proved just that. She was ahead and seemed to have it all tied up with 30 metres left, but all those sessions with Chell, working on mechanics and not losing energy through bad technique, paid off. I crossed the line in 22.83 seconds, a lifetime best. Dafne was given the win even though we clocked the same time. After day one I had 4158 points. That was a lead of 184 from Austra Skujyte, with Jessica Zelinka third. Chernova was 309 points adrift, double the deficit she made up in Daegu, and Dobrynska was 323 behind. It was my best first day by 34 points and some 45 up on the total I'd posted in Götzis when I'd broken the British record in May. The numbers added up. I felt I was on my way.

I went through the press mixed zone. Chell wanted to get me through as quickly as possible because he wanted to get me checked over by Ali and Derry. My warm-down was a power-walk through the tunnel to the warm-up track. There were lots of smiles.

'You're in great shape, Jess,' Ali said.

Derry took over with his magic hands and gave me a flush-through and an ice massage. 'You're doing great.'

We had some dinner with Kat. An American athlete came over and asked for a picture.

'Oh my God, you're amazing,' he said.

Then he turned to Kat. 'And your name is hilarious.'

It seemed a random thing to say and clearly he had not much experience of double-barrelled names. I rang Andy but the phone died. I texted Mum at close to midnight, saying I was sorry I had not got to speak to her.

The heptathlon wipes you – the adrenaline, the effort, the pain, the concentration and even the hours. Normally, I'd go to bed at home around 10 p.m. but the days of competition are long and exacting. And now I was facing the longest day of my life.

I tried not to fill my head with too much doubt, but by the time I'd got back to my room, after having treatment, an ice massage, and food, it was midnight. Normally I switch off quickly, but I still couldn't sleep. My legs were restless and I lay there tossing and turning. It was such a huge moment. Everything was on it and it was so different to anything else I'd ever done. I didn't go out to the balcony and look at the stadium, and I didn't want to look back either. My mind and muscles were twitching and I remember waking myself up by kicking out at the wall. I don't know what Kate Dennison in the next-door room must have thought was going on.

I woke up at 6 a.m. and felt totally drained. It was emotional. I felt very tired due to the lack of sleep, and thought it was not great to be feeling this way with what lay ahead. I went to get some fresh air and have breakfast. I needed coffee. So did the two figures that I saw in the dining hall, bags packed. They had finished competing and had clearly been out the night before. It showed how everyone was living to different schedules. They were stumbling around after a finishing a night of drinking, while I awaited the most serious moments of my life.

I still knew I could mess it up. Of course I did. I knew there was so much that could go wrong, especially when the first event of the day was the long jump. The lead over Chernova was big, but she had a best of over 6.80 metres in the long jump. If she matched that and I jumped around 6.10 metres then she would claw back more than 200 points. If we both matched our bests in the javelin she would then take another 150 points off me. It did not take a stretch of the imagination to believe that she could comfortably overhaul me.

Chell was good in these circumstances. He was calm, but sometimes he says things that get me riled.

'You have 80,000 friends out there,' he told me before every event. I knew it was a cheesy ritual for him, but it worked too. When you are in that stressful situation, it's anything that gets you through, for both of us.

It could all be undone in the long jump and I struggled in the warm-up. I was a bit over the board, which is a foul, and so I discussed it with Chell. He said I should move my run-up back at bit. One more shoe. I actually moved it a couple of extra feet without him knowing. In all it went back seven feet, a huge amount on the day of an Olympic final. It was a massive gamble. You have to listen to your coach but you also have to listen to yourself. Chernova's first jump was 6.44 metres and mine was an abject 5.95 metres. The points difference between those two was 140 points. I was a third of the way to the nightmare scenario. I was panicking. I was glad not to have got a no-jump, but I was fixating on the runway. Now I needed to really jump. I went to see Chell who came down to the front row of the stand. That was hard because I was trying to have a shouted in-depth discussion with my coach, while hordes of people next to him were shouting: 'Jess, Jess, Jess.' I was trying to block out all the people taking pictures because I knew my whole world could fall apart in the next few minutes and all those pictures would be deleted.

Mum, Dad, Mel and Andy were in the stadium. As it turned out their seats were in my long-jump eye line. Unbeknown to me they moved somewhere else because they knew they would distract me. I would smile at them and they didn't want that, so they moved and found somewhere to watch in anonymity. I was so glad they did.

Chernova improved to 6.54 metres with her second jump. Then it was my time. I ran freely, hit the board and hung. The days, months and even years of agony in the long jump, rebuilding the event after breaking my ankle and all of 2012's traumas, came down to these few seconds. I reached, landed and bounced up. It looked good, but I waited, expectantly but tentatively.

6.40 metres

I had ticked it off. More than anything I had averted a calamity. Maybe it got to Chernova because she could not improve on her last jump, whereas I, with the comfort of knowing I was in the box seat, increased mine to 6.48

metres. A crucial event that could have wrecked my dream was done and dusted.

There were two events left. The javelin, the reason I'd lost the world title in Daegu, and the 800 metres, the most painful event of all. I knew the javelin was not a major problem. Some people had hyped it up into being a real issue, but I believed Daegu was a one-off. I had been consistent all year and felt confident. I never doubted Mick. I knew that he was the man who was capable of me getting there. I felt I needed a personal best, and when I threw 46.61 metres with my first attempt I felt emotional. There was a sudden sensation that I was almost home, but I quashed it as quickly as it came.

Then I increased my distance to 47.49 metres, the personal best I craved and needed. Chernova, despite throwing more than 54 metres in the past, could not match it. Dobrynska had already gone, three no-jumps in the long jump convincing her to quit. She was one of five women who had started the competition to have pulled out, testament to the fact the heptathlon is gruelling and saps both mind and body, leaving you physically screaming with hurt whether it goes well or not.

I was 188 points clear of Skujyte. Chernova was sixth. Kat was now nineteenth but still relishing every moment. For me it was not enjoyable. I could not enjoy it for more than a few fleeting nanoseconds with so much at stake. People say the journey should be as satisfying as the destination, but it wasn't. I came off the track after the javelin and I was fighting back the tears because I knew I was so close to the end. The team were there and they were relaxed. Mick kept saying, 'You're going to do it', which had been like a mantra throughout. Chell was relaxed and chatting away but I could sense his excitement. Mike Holmes, Kat's coach, was there too.

'It's not over yet,' I told them. 'It's not over.'

Mick listened, ignored me and broke out into a big smile.

'Yeah, but how are we going to celebrate?'

I asked Chell if he could work it out. He rolled his eyes.

'Seriously? You're going to make me work out all the figures.'

'Yes, I need to know.'

So he did.

The gaps were huge. I could finish fifteen seconds behind Skujyte and win. I had twenty seconds over Lyudmyla Yosypenko in third and, significantly, twenty-five seconds on Chernova. The figures were music to my ears and confidence oozed through me.

'Do you want me to keep going?' Chell asked.

The 800 metres was scheduled to start at 8.35 p.m. but I was going to be in the last heat, sandwiched between the long-jump and 10,000 metres finals. It was a long wait because I wanted to run the race now. Get it over with. Kill the pressure. The television set in the combined events room switched to the studio where Denise Lewis and Michael Johnson began discussing me. I put my fingers in my ears and ran out of the room. I didn't want to hear what they were saying. 'Tell me afterwards,' I thought.

I went to the warm-up track and saw Mo preparing for the 10,000 metres. Mo had taken a different path to me. Born in Somalia, raised in Djibouti and now living in America, where he was trained by a Cuban-born coach, he had travelled the world to get to London. I had stayed in Sheffield with the coach I had had since junior school. Different paths to the same goal. I wished him well and he did the same.

I watched Dai Greene's 400 metres hurdles semi-final on the television. He struggled home in fourth place but just got through into the final. He looked devastated and it showed how sometimes things do not quite go as you have imagined for months on end. The clock ticked. There were other heptathletes warming up and trying to get their bodies to hold together for one last act. Then we were led through the tunnel into the stadium once more. I was in the last heat along with the other top-ranked girls. This heat featured the athletes lying in the top positions after six events, so would decide the medal places. Chernova towered over me as we were led away. She was in lane three and I was in four.

We were led along the side of the track to the start. The girls from the last heat had just finished and were dying on the red floor. It was not a nice feeling to have to step over people, as they were scraped off the track, to get to your lane. It filled me with pure fear.

This is it. I want to get to the front and I am going to go out a bit too hard just to stay out of trouble. I don't want to be tripped or spiked or elbowed by 'those big girls'. I am really close to it now. I can almost taste it, and yet it also seems so far, far away. I don't look around, or think about the journey. I don't think about the flames of the Sheffield steelworks, or the orange fire away to my right. I banish all emotion and think about forging a triumph here and now.

The gun. Accelerate. Faster. Flashbulbs. A dull roar. I hit the front

My plan is to get through the first lap in sixty-one seconds. I can hear the noise from the crowd. It is sending shudders through me yet I feel comfortable. The bell sounds. One lap. Little more than one minute to complete a sixteen-year race. I don't want to push too hard because I don't want to blow up. On the back straight Lilli Schwarzkopf overhauls me. She edges in front and then Chernova also comes past. I can feel Jessica Zelinka closing too as we round the last bend. I think, 'I've run harder than this in training.' I push through the lactic. I have no choice but to run wide as we come into the home straight to get past. It's my only way past Schwarzkopf and Chernova. Tactically it is not great, but you have to find a way.

As I move forwards I hear the crowd erupt. I feel I am being carried along. Close now. It is just another home straight but it is a foreign and alien one. Then I think back to Götzis when Chernova beat me in the 800 metres. Then she said that she knew I'd won but at least she had beaten me in the 800. It was a badge of honour. I thought fleetingly of Daegu and the photograph of her finishing the 800 metres there and celebrating as my face dropped. I had thought about that picture many times in the past year. I am not going to let her have the last bit of glory. There are no consolation prizes. I want to put on a show and thank the crowd for their support. I want it to be a great finish to the two days and I want that feeling of crossing the line first. So I run and run and I win. I am the Olympic champion.

14

AFTERMATH

I don't remember putting my arms out in a wide, Y-shaped victory salute. I never celebrate like that. I rarely celebrate at all because I feel too reserved. I fell to the floor and the tears came. You will be aware by now that I cry a lot, but rarely in public. However, this time the floodgates opened and the relief just poured out of me. The cameras clicked and then I sat up and took the congratulations of some of the other girls. I had won my heat in 2 minutes 8.65 seconds. Jessica Zelinka had come through into second place. The scoreboard said Lilli had been disqualified but I was oblivious to that. I went to find Chell. He tried to get down from the stand to embrace me. I held out a hand across the gap to him but we couldn't quite reach each other. He shrugged. Derry threw a big Union Jack flag at me that had 'Jessica Ennis – Olympic champion' printed on it. That amazed me. Later

I told him: 'You must have had some faith in me to have that made.' He said: 'Don't worry, if you'd lost you'd never have known about it.'

As usual we all went on our lap of honour together. We held hands and bowed to the crowd on the back straight. Mum and Dad had rushed down to the side of the track on the home straight but I didn't see them. I was unaware at that point that what people would call the greatest night in British athletics – some would even say in British sport – was unfolding. I won at 9.04 p.m. Greg won the long jump at 9.26 p.m., by which time Mo was a few laps into the 10,000 metres final. When he won in the most dramatic fashion we had three gold medals in less than 45 minutes. Given that we had only won one gold medal in Beijing, it was an incredible gold rush.

I came off the track and Phil Jones was there as usual for the BBC. He grabbed me and, when he mentioned the journey I had been on since Beijing, the tears came again. I edged away, rubbed my eyes and tried to compose myself, but I had never experienced emotions quite like it. I found it hard to stop.

Then, as I was coming through the mixed zone, an official who had a finger in one ear and an earpiece on stopped me. He was listening to a message.

'Hang on a minute, Jessica,' he said. 'There's been a protest.'

My heart dropped like a stone. I thought, 'Oh my God, that would be just typical, wouldn't it?'

I asked him what it was about. He listened a bit more. I thought: I've celebrated too early again. This would be the ultimate kick in the teeth if they took it away from me now. I'd even done a lap of honour this time. They were awful, never-ending seconds.

'It's about stepping out of lane,' he said.

I thought, I definitely haven't done that.

'It's nothing to do with you,' he said, and I broke out into another smile, the relief heaped on relief. It turned out that the Germans had appealed after Lilli Schwarzkopf had been disqualified. She was reinstated because it emerged that the officials had made a mistake and confused her with the Ukrainian in the next lane. Ukraine appealed. In the end it meant that I won with a new British record, 6955 points.

Lilli was second, 306 points behind. Chernova was third. I had beaten her by a huge distance.

Finally, I made it to the combined events room and the team were there. I had never seen Chell so excited. This time he gave me a proper bear hug. There was no awkwardness or embarrassed pat. It was a hug of 'I can't breathe' proportions. We had done it.

The medal ceremony was that night. You sit in a room with the medallists, waiting your turn. Seb Coe came in and said hello. He had presented me with my silver medal in Daegu. Back then he told me he was going to put his name down to present the heptathlon medals in London which 'you will win'. He too comes from Sheffield – he had great belief in me and he had done so much to make the Olympics happen that it seemed fitting.

Sometimes the stadiums empty before the ceremonies, or they are held so early or late that nobody is there. This time the place was full. I saw Andy and wondered why he had sunglasses on and then realized how emotional it was for him too. As we were led out I could hear David Bowie's 'Heroes' being played over the tannoy and I felt myself welling up again. I walked out and Carmel was leaning over the side of the tunnel, tears in her eyes, screaming, 'Yeahhhh.' I had always felt that it would be a really hard battle, that things would go wrong and that there would be the ultimate disappointment, so I could not believe that it had all gone to plan. That was the sensation as the National Anthem played, I crumbled again and the crowd sang along. It all seemed totally unbelievable to me.

I still had drug testing to do. The last race of the night had been the women's 100 metres final. Allyson Felix, of the USA, was in there. She had finished fifth and was disappointed. We watched a TV screen showing the highlights. She said congratulations and I told her that she still had the 200 metres. She looked crestfallen in that room but would leave London with three gold medals.

That's what sport gives you – slaps in the face and then slaps on the back. You have to come back from taking punishment to be a champion.

It was around midnight when I left the stadium and headed for Team GB house, a building next to the huge Westfield shopping centre on the edge of the park. It was here that the British Olympic Association had its headquarters during the Games and they set rooms aside for the medallists and their families. That was where we had our reunion. We had a glass of champagne but the thing I remembered most was how much weight Dad had lost. I thought he was ill and asked Mum if they had been keeping something horrible from me. She said he had been poorly but said he had not eaten for days and that it was down to stress. It had taken its toll on them all. Everyone was excited when we realized the gold medal was missing.

'Where is it? Where is it?'

We had a moment of panic before someone noticed Grandma was sitting down with it and looking at it. When I finally got back to the village, my roomies had left notes on my door. One of them said, 'You made me cry.' At least it was not just me.

I had not eaten since 3 p.m. that afternoon and crashed out. I was entered for the hurdles and had to say whether I was taking my place by the following morning. I decided not to. I wanted to savour the moment and I couldn't have done that if I'd been preparing for another event. My time from my hurdles heat might have won gold in the solo event in Beijing, but it wouldn't have in London because I was wrecked. My body had taken a pounding. I had really only entered as a back-up, in case the heptathlon had gone wrong and I needed a chance to make amends. I was not keeping anyone else out of the team so I had no hesitation in saying I was done.

The next day I celebrated with a burger and chips as I did no end of interviews. I appeared on NBC with Bruce Jenner and met Jamie Oliver, and I was introduced to 35,000 people in Hyde Park by Johnny Vaughan. I thanked all my team and family and then mentioned my fiancé. That drew a chorus of disapproval and wholesale booing. We talked some more and I mentioned the 'f' word again. More boos. I turned to Andy, hiding at the back of the stage, and laughed. Then I blew him a kiss. I stayed in London for that week and watched some of the sport. I was so pleased for the boxers, Anthony Joshua and Nicola Adams, who did well. I knew them because I trained alongside them in the gym at the EIS.

Suddenly, we were being invited everywhere. During that week Andy and I went to an underground Stone Roses gig organized by Adidas and attended an Omega party where I got to wear a gorgeous Alexander McQueen dress and have a celebration dinner with Team Ennis. The fun times were here.

I came back to Sheffield on a high. A lot of people had said that there is a sense of anti-climax when you finally reach your goal, that attaining all you'd ever wanted left a strange feeling of emptiness. I was glad to find I did not experience that at all. I could not stop smiling and felt enormous satisfaction and pride. I knew it was the best time of my life and that nothing would ever top it. I now wished that I could have dragged it out and savoured it, because I knew I had wished it all away.

We had a barbecue for friends and family at home. Charlotte was heavily pregnant, but she came and danced away to Andy's mounting concern that she was about to have the baby there and then.

The momentum carried on. There was a reception for me in Sheffield city centre and I was blown away by the number of people who turned up. After I'd won the world title there had been a few hundred in the Peace Gardens, and I'd felt humbled by that. This time everybody seemed to go and thousands flocked to City Hall. My friend Lorna works in a solicitor's in town and said everybody had been let go early. There was a note on the door of someone else's workplace saying: 'We're closed. We're going to support Jessica.' I have since been awarded the freedom of the City. I am going to have to find out what that entitles me to, but I believe I might be able to drive sheep through the city centre.

Andy and I took a holiday in Mauritius and people kept congratulating me even there. Meanwhile, the Paralympics were taking place, stretching people's imaginations even more and continuing the best summer I'd ever had. When they finished there was the parade for all the Olympic and Paralympic athletes in London on 10 September. That was an astonishing sight. It made you realize how a very personal quest could capture the interest of other people. I knew the Olympics were going to be big, but I did not realize it had touched so many people and that there was so much emotion invested in it. From the average bloke in the street to the Royal Family, and from school-kids to celebrities, everyone seemed to have been sucked into this incredible festival.

At the parade I saw Anthony Joshua, who also had his gold medal. He is a super-heavyweight boxer, a huge figure, and that was exaggerated as he stood next to me. We were joking with each other and I said to him: 'Joshua, I will knock you out.' He tapped me gently on the arm and I nearly fell over. Richard Whitehead had won a gold medal in the sprinting at the Paralympics. He stood next to me on our float and was flexing his muscles in the Tarzan pose.

'Come on Jess, you do it.'

I told him I would not be doing that. I didn't fancy that being the picture they printed in the papers the next day, and so I let him flex away.

Life had become strange. I did not feel famous, but I was asked to be in Robbie Williams's music video – I had to turn it down – and I would hear kids walking down the road, saying: 'That's Jessica Ennis's house.' People drive past and point. The day after winning the gold medal, a journalist asked Andy if he was ready for the change in our lives. 'Well, I guess we won't be doing a big shop together for a while,' he deadpanned. And we didn't. I was self-conscious about going out because I would feel people staring at me. I didn't go into the city centre for a long time. It was all so overwhelming.

Thirty-six days after winning gold, I got in the car and drove to the EIS. I had the urge to go training, to do something. I had drunk enough and eaten enough bad food and felt the need to get back to running. I had the wedding to plan for and will want to have kids one day, but I was already beginning to think about a new plan. Who knows whether I will carry on to Rio or switch to becoming a specialist hurdler in the future, but thirty-six days after my golden moment, I was a heptathlete again.

I believe we all have a journey. It may be in sport or something completely different. I receive so many letters from young people that I hope are inspired by what I have done. I do not mean that they have to become Olympians, but just to find what they want to do and then not let the setbacks along the way grind them down and make them give up. I was once a small girl from Sheffield, dealing with bullies and normal teenage insecurities, but I always believed. And when you do that, life can get unbelievable.

Jessica Ennis

CAREER STATISTICS

Compiled by Alan Lindop

Scoring and regulations

Points for both the Women's Pentathlon and Heptathlon are scored from the IAAF Scoring Tables. The current (1984) tables came into force on 1 April 1985. The tables take into consideration times taken with manually timed performances and electrically timed marks. World-leading heptathletes usually score in the region of 6300 points plus.

Listed overleaf are examples of performances which would score 1000 points per discipline and 800 points per discipline, as well as the world record and Jessica's Olympic winning score.

Example scores

Event	1000 Pts	800 Pts	World Record (7291)	Jessica ENNIS (6955)
100mh	13.65s	15.32s	12.69 –1172	12.54 – 1195
HJ	1.82 (1003)	1.66 (806)	1.86 – 1054	1.86 – 1054
SP	17.07	14.09	15.80 – 915	14.28 – 813
200m	23.80s	25.97s	22.56 – 1123	22.83 – 1096
LJ	6.48 (1001)	5.84 (801)	7.27 – 1264	6.48 – 1001
JT	57.18	46.87	45.66 – 776	47.49 – 812
800m	2:07.63	2:21.77	2:08.51 – 987	2:08.65 – 984

In the shot, long jump and javelin each athlete is allowed three trials only. In the 100m hurdles and 200m, athletes with similar performances are placed in the same heats, but the 800m race is determined from the positions of the previous six events so that the last heat comprises the leading competitors. Where possible thirty minutes should be allowed between the end of one event and the start of the subsequent event. Under present rules one false start is allowed without the athlete being disqualified but any subsequent false start by the same athlete and she will be disqualified. Any athlete failing to attempt to start or make a trial in one of the events shall not be allowed to take part in any subsequent event but shall be considered to have abandoned the competition. This is distinct from athletes failing to record a distance (e.g. three no-jumps or three no-throws) or record a height having attempted it. For records the average velocity of the wind shall not exceed 2.0 miles per second (mps).

Abbreviations

OS	Olympic Stadium	HJ	high jump
SC	Stadium City	SP	shot put
i	indoor	200m	200 metres
w	Wind assisted	LJ	long jump
100mh	100 metre hurdles	JT	javelin throw
60mh	60 metre hurdles	800m	800 metres

Full career record of Combined events
up to 4 August 2012

Senior Heptathlon

100mh/mps	HJ	SP	200m/mps	LJ/mps	JT	800m	Pts	Pos
AAA Junior Championships, Bedford, 15 Jul 01								
14.60/1.7	1.67	9.04	25.25/0.1	5.20/2.1	22.52	2:28.12	4711	3
v FRA, GER, ITA, SUI, Bedford, 05 Aug 01								
14.53/1.5	1.72	8.67	25.55/2.0	5.24/0.8	23.57	2:25.04	4801	9
AAA Junior Championships, Wrexham, 23 Jun 02								
15.23/-4.1	1.77	9.17	24.72/1.7	5.21/1.9	22.84	2:26.44	4837	2
v SUI, FRA, GER, Pratteln, 04 Aug 02								
14.32/0.6	1.74	9.21	24.52/2.5	5.63/0.0	26.54	2:21.84	5194	2
Multistars Meeting, Desenzano, 11 May 03								
14.02/0.6	1.61	9.79	24.44/-0.5	5.52/0.9	26.82	2:20.20	5116	13
Multistars Meeting, Desenzano, 09 May 04								
14.10/-1.6	1.79	10.27	24.42/0.4	5.52/-0.7	24.87	2:17.34	5364	12
World Junior Championships, Grosseto, 17 Jul 04								
13.57/0.6	1.80	10.52	24.23/-0.3	5.59/0.3	28.04	2:19.16	5542	8
Multistars Meeting, Salo, 08 May 05								
13.82/0.1	1.85	11.88	24.79/-3.3	6.09/-0.3	30.28	2:17.03	5827	4
European Junior Championships, Kaunas, 24 Jul 05								
13.46/-2.0	1.79	11.40	24.29/-0.9	6.19/-0.9	32.55	2:17.23	5891	1
World University Games, Izmir, 16 Aug 05								
13.56/-1.1	1.87	12.26	24.43/0.6	6.22/-1.0	28.94	2:21.08	5910	3
Commonwealth Games, Melbourne, 22 Mar 06								
13.32/2.0	1.91	11.87	23.80/0.9	6.15/-0.1	36.39	2:12.66	6269	3

100mh/mps	HJ	SP	200m/mps	LJ/mps	JT	800m	Pts	Pos
European Cup C/E Super League, Arles, 02 Jul 06								
13.37/2.2	1.86	12.36	23.76/1.3	6.12/0.0	36.81	2:16.95	6170	4
European Championships, Gothenburg, 08 Aug 06								
13.33/1.0	1.86	12.72	23.56/0.2	6.18/0.5	36.65	2:13.45	6287	8
Multistars Meeting, Desenzano, 06 May 07								
13.12/0.2	1.95	12.13	23.68/0.6	6.40/-0.3	33.91	2:14.31	6388	1
European Cup C/E Super League, Szczecin, 08 Jul 07								
13.05/0.9	1.87	12.89	23.65/3.1	6.20/2.5	37.38	2:10.91	6399	1
World Championships, Osaka, 26 Aug 07								
12.97/0.1	1.89	11.93	23.15/0.3	6.33/0.1	38.07	2:11.39	6469	4
Hypo International Meeting, Götzis, 01 Jun 08								
13.36/-1.1	1.85	13.52	23.59/1.8	withdrew	withdrew	withdrew	Dnf	-
Multistars Meeting, Desenzano, 10 May 09								
12.98/0.7	1.90	13.19	23.49/-0.5	6.16/-0.4	42.70	2:09.88	6587	1
World Championships, Berlin, 16 Aug 09								
12.93/-0.4	1.92	14.14	23.25/0.0	6.29/-0.8	43.54	2:12.22	6731	1
Hypo International Meeting, Götzis, 30 May 10								
12.89/0.7	1.91	14.25	23.31/1.0	6.13/0.3	43.40	2:11.19	6689	1
European Championships, Barcelona, 31 Jul 10								
12.95/-1.0	1.89	14.05	23.21/-0.3	6.43/1.1	46.71	2:10.18	6823	1
Hypo International Meeting, Götzis, 29 May 11								
13.03/0.0	1.91	13.94	23.11/1.8	6.37/0.5	43.83	2:08.46	6790	1
World Championships, Daegu, 30 Aug 11								
12.94/0.4	1.86	14.67	23.27/-1.5	6.51/0.0	39.95	2:07.81	6751	2
Hypo International Meeting, Götzis, 27 May 12								
12.81/0.0	1.85	14.51	22.88/1.9	6.51/0.8	47.11	2:09.00	6906	1
Olympic Games, London(OS), 04 Aug 12								
12.54/1.3	1.86	14.28	22.83/-0.3	6.48/-0.6	47.49	2:08.65	6955	1

25 Senior Heptathlons

Indoor Pentathlon

60mh	HJ	SP	LJ	800m	Pts	Pos
v FRA, ESP (U20 International), Eaubonne, 24 Feb 02						
8.76	1.74	8.55	5.39	2:30.44	3654	5
v FRA. ESP (U20 International), Cardiff, 26 Jan 03						
8.78	1.76	9.06	5.55	2:28.03	3785	2
AAA Junior Indoor Championships, Cardiff, 23 Mar 03						
8.76	1.75	9.43	5.29	2:28.63	3719	1
AAA Indoor Championships, Cardiff, 13 Mar 05						
8.48	1.80	10.49	5.64	2:22.75	4089	1
v FRA, ESP (U23 International), Eaubonne, 25 Feb 06						
8.29	1.87	11.82	5.85	2:20.45	4401	1
European Indoor Championships, Birmingham, 02 Mar 07						
8.22	1.91	13.28	6.19	2:17.03	4716	6
World Indoor Championships, Doha, 13 Mar 10						
8.04	1.90	14.01	6.44	2:12.55	4937	1
World Indoor Championships, Istanbul, 09 Mar 12						
7.91	1.87	14.79	6.19	2:08.09	4965	2

8 Senior Pentathlons

Other Combined events competitions

Under 15 Pentathlon

60mh/mps	HJ	SP	LJ	800m	Pts	Pos
English Schools – NE Region, Sheffield, 27 Jun 99						
12.2	1.51	6.55	4.40	2:32.7	2652	2
AAA Under 15 Championships, Stoke-on-Trent, 22 Aug 99						
12.48/-4.3	1.60	6.89	4.67/0.7	2:43.96	2686	4
English Schools Final, Peterborough, 19 Sep 99						
11.65/1.5	1.60	6.75	4.38/2.2	2:54.06	2591	15
AAA Under 15 Championships, Stoke-on-Trent, 18 Jun 00						
11.68/-3.2	1.69	7.92	5.34	2:45.95	3109	1

Under 17 Heptathlon with 80m Hurdles

80mh	HJ	SP	200m	LJ	JT	800m	Pts	Pos
English Schools – NE Region, Jarrow, 24 Jun 01								
12.4	1.75	9.06	25.4	5.01	18.22	2:27.4	4504	1
English Schools Final, Hull, 16 Sep 01								
12.11	1.75	8.59	26.61	5.22	22.78	2:29.95	4538	2

Under 18 Heptathlon with 100m Hurdles

100mh/mps	HJ	SP	200m/mps	LJ	JT	800m	Pts	Pos
World Youth Championships, Sherbrooke, 13 Jul 03								
13.86/0.6	1.75	10.13	24.56/-3.0	5.47/-0.2	25.52	2:18.21	5311	5

Triathlon

SP	LJ/mps	100mh/mps	Points	Position
Grand Prix Meeting, New York, 12 Jun 10				
13.61	6.51/0.7	12.85/1.3	2925	2

Indoor Triathlon (Long Jump, Shot Put, 60m Hurdles)

LJ	SP	60mh	Points	Position
City Challenge Event, Cardiff, 28 Feb 09				
5.98	12.99	8.25	2643	1

Major International Championships

	Competition	Position	Event
2003	World Youth Championships	5th	Heptathlon
2004	World Junior Championships	8th	Heptathlon
	Commonwealth Youth	2nd	100mh
		2nd	HJ
2005	European Junior Championships	1st	Heptathlon
	World University Games	3rd	Heptathlon
2006	Commonwealth Games	3rd	Heptathlon
	European Cup C/E Super League	4th	Heptathlon
	European Championships	8th	Heptathlon
2007	European Indoors	6th	Pentathlon
	European Cup C/E Super League	1st	Heptathlon
	Member of winning GB Team for the first time		
	European Under 23 Championships	3rd	100mh
	World Championships	4th	Heptathlon
2009	World Championships	1st	Heptathlon
2010	World Indoors	1st	Pentathlon
	European Championships	1st	Heptathlon
2011	World Championships	2nd	Heptathlon
2012	World Indoor Championships	1st	Pentathlon
	Olympic Games	1st	Heptathlon

United Kingdom Championships

	Position	Event
2007	1st	HJ(i)
	3rd	60mh(i)
	3rd	LJ(i)
	1st	100mh(i)
	1st	HJ(i)
2008	1st	HJ(i)
	3rd	60mh(i)
2009	1st	100mh
	1st	HJ
2011	1st	HJ(i)
	1st	HJ(i)
	2nd	100mh(i)
	3rd	LJ(i)
2012	1st	60mh(i)
	1st	HJ(i)
	1st	HJ(i)
	1st	100mh(i)

AAA/England Championships

	Competition	Position	Event
1999	U15 Girls	2nd	HJ
		4th	Pent
2000	U15 Girls Indoors	1st	HJ(i)
		2nd	60mh(i)
	U15 Girls	1st	HJ
		1st	Pent
		2nd	75mh
2001	U17 Indoors	2nd	60mh(i)
		10th	LJ(i)
	U17	2nd	HJ
		4th	80mh
	U20	3rd	Heptathlon
2002	U20	2nd	Heptathlon
		4th	100mh
2003	U20 Indoors	1st	Pentathlon(i)
	U20	1st	100mh
2004	Senior Indoor	8th	60mh(i)
2005	Senior Indoor	1st	Pentathlon(i)
	Senior	3rd	100mh
2006	Senior Indoor	5th	60mh(i)
	Senior	3rd	HJ
		4th	100mh
	U23	2nd	LJ
2007	U23	1st	100mh

English Schools Championships

	Competition	Position	Event
1999	U15	10th 15th	HJ Pentathlon
2000	U15	1st	HJ
2001	U17	2nd 2nd	HJ Heptathlon
2002	U17	1st	HJ

BREAKDOWN OF KEY CAREER EVENTS
Commonwealth Games, Melbourne, 22 Mar 06

Event	Result	Position	Points	Overall
100 metres hurdles	13.32s	3rd	1077	3rd
High jump	1.91m	1st	1119	1st
Shot put	11.87m	8th	653	2nd
200 metres	23.80s	3rd	1000	2nd
Long jump	6.15m	5th	896	2nd
Javelin	36.39m	9th	598	2nd
800 metres	2:12.66s	5th	926	3rd
TOTAL			6269	3rd

European Championships, Gothenburg, 08 Aug 06

Event	Result	Position	Points	Overall
100 metres hurdles	13.33s	4th	1075	4th
High jump	1.86m	4th	1054	3rd
Shot put	12.72m	19th	709	6th
200 metres	23.56s	1st	1023	3rd
Long jump	6.19m	11th	908	4th
Javelin	36.65m	23rd	603	7th
800 metres	2:13.45s	7th	915	8th
TOTAL			6287	8th

European Indoor Championships, Birmingham, 02 Mar 07

Event	Result	Position	Points	Overall
60 metres hurdles	8.22s	2nd	1079	2nd
High jump	1.91m	1st	1119	1st
Shot put	13.28m	10th	746	5th
Long jump	6.19m	9th	908	6th
800 metres	2:17.03s	9th	864	6th
TOTAL			4716	6th

World Championships, Osaka, 26 Aug 07

Event	Result	Position	Points	Overall
100 metres hurdles	12.97s	1st	1129	1st
High jump	1.89m	3rd	1093	2nd
Shot put	11.93m	34th	656	4th
200 metres	23.15s	1st	1064	4th
Long jump	6.33m	9th	953	4th
Javelin	38.07m	26th	630	5th
800 metres	2:11.39s	1st	944	4th
TOTAL			6469	4th

World Championships, Berlin, 16 Aug 09

Event	Result	Position	Points	Overall
100 metres hurdles	12.93s	1st	1135	1st
High jump	1.92m	1st	1132	1st
Shot put	14.14m	5th	803	1st
200 metres	23.25s	1st	1054	1st
Long jump	6.29m	9th	940	1st
Javelin	43.54m	10th	735	1st
800 metres	2:12.22s	1st	932	1st
TOTAL			6731	1st

World Indoor Championships, Doha, 13 Mar 10

Event	Result	Position	Points	Overall
60 metres hurdles	8.04s	1st	1120	1st
High jump	1.90m	1st	1106	1st
Shot put	14.01m	5th	795	1st
Long jump	6.44m	3rd	988	1st
800 metres	2:12.55s	2nd	928	1st
TOTAL			4937	1st

European Championships, Barcelona, 31 Jul 10

Event	Result	Position	Points	Overall
100 metres hurdles	12.95s	1st	1132	1st
High jump	1.89m	1st	1093	1st
Shot put	14.05m	6th	797	1st
200 metres	23.21s	1st	1058	1st
Long jump	6.43m	4th	985	1st
Javelin	46.71m	8th	796	1st
800 metres	2:10.18s	1st	962	1st
TOTAL			6823	1st

World Championships, Daegu, 30 Aug 11

Event	Result	Position	Points	Overall
100 metres hurdles	12.94s	2nd	1133	2nd
High jump	1.86m	2nd	1054	2nd
Shot put	14.67m	7th	839	1st
200 metres	23.27s	1st	1052	1st
Long jump	6.51m	2nd	1010	1st
Javelin	39.95m	21st	666	2nd
800 metres	2:07.8 s	2nd	997	2nd
TOTAL			6751	2nd

World Indoor Championships, Istanbul, 09 Mar 12

Event	Result	Position	Points	Overall
60 metres hurdles	7.91s	1st	1150	1st
High jump	1.87m	3rd	1067	1st
Shot put	14.79m	4th	847	1st
Long jump	6.19m	7th	908	3rd
800 metres	2:08.09s	1st	993	2nd
TOTAL			4965	2nd

Olympic Games, London, 04 Aug 12

Event	Result	Position	Points	Overall
100 metres hurdles	12.54s	1st	1195	1st
High jump	1.86m	5th	1054	1st
Shot put	14.28m	9th	813	2nd
200 metres	22.83s	1st	1096	1st
Long jump	6.48m	2nd	1001	1st
Javelin	47.49m	10th	812	1st
800 metres	2:08.65s	1st	984	1st
TOTAL		1st	6955	1st

Personal best performances
up to 4 August 2012

60m indoors	7.36	Sheffield	16 Jan 10
100m	11.68 (-1.2)	Manchester(SC)	20 Jun 09
150m	16.99 (+0.4)	Manchester	16 May 10
200m	22.83 (-0.3)	London (OS)	03 Aug 12
800m	2:07.81	Daegu	30 Aug 11
60m hurdles indoors	7.87	Birmingham	18 Feb 12
100m hurdles	12.54 (+1.3)	London (OS)	03 Aug 12
High jump	1.95	Desenzano	06 May 07
Long jump	6.54w (+2.4)	Manchester	02 Jun 07
	6.51 (+0.7)	New York	12 Jun 10
	6.51 (0.0)	Daegu	30 Aug 11
	6.51 (+0.8)	Götzis	27 May 12
Shot put	14.79i	Istanbul	09 Mar 12
	14.67	Daegu	29 Aug 11
Javelin	47.49	London (OS)	04 Aug 12
Pentathlon indoors	4965p	Istanbul	09 Mar 12
Heptathlon	6955p	London (OS)	04 Aug 12

United Kingdom records set by Jessica Ennis
up to 4 August 2012

Senior Heptathlon

| 6906 | Götzis | 26/27 May 2012 | (also Commonwealth record) |
| 6955 | London (OS) | 03/04 Aug 2012 | (also Commonwealth record) |

100 metres Hurdles

| 12.54 | London (OS) | 03 Aug 2012 |

High Jump

| 1.95 | Desenzano | 05 May 2007 | (equalled record) |

Series: 1.74 (o), 1.77 (o), 1.80 (o), 1.83 (o), 1.86 (o), 1.89 (xo), 1.92 (o), 1.95 (xo), 198 (xxx)

Indoor 60 metres Hurdles

| 7.95s | Glasgow | 30 Jan 2010 |

Indoor Pentathlon

| 4937 | Doha | 13 Mar 2010 | (also Commonwealth best) |
| 4965 | Istanbul | 09 Mar 2012 | (also Commonwealth best) |

- Jessica's 12.54s set at the Olympics was the best performance in the world in a heptathlon event. She also holds the United Kingdom best performances in a heptathlon in the high jump (1.95m), 200 metres (22.83s).

- Jessica's best marks in a heptathlon are 12.54s (100mh), 1.95 (HJ), 14.67 (SP), 22.83 (200m), 6.54w/6.51 (LJ), 47.49 (JT), 2:07.81 (800m).

- If Jessica achieved personal bests in all her heptathlon events her score would be 7138 points (with windy LJ/indoor SP).

- The average of Jessica's top 10 heptathlons is 6710 pts.

- Jessica finished runner up in the 2007 IAAF World Combined Events Challenge and in the same year won the European Athletic Association Rising Star Award.

- As of 1 October 2012 Jessica ranks number 5 on the World All Time Ranking behind:

Jackie Joyner-Kersee (7291p)
Carolina Klüft (7032p)
Larisa Turchinskaya (7007p)
Sabine Braun (6985p).

INDEX

AAA Championship (2005) 49
Adams, Valerie 219–20
Adidas 118, 138–9, 145, 193, 194, 238
Ahmed, Fuzz 205
Alexander Stadium, Birmingham 195–7
Athens Olympic Games (2004) 90
Aviva 193
Aviva Grand Prix (2010/2012) 122, 177
Aviva International Match (2011) 143
Aviva Startrack camp 21–2, 23, 26

Barcelona European Championships (2010) 125–6, 128–32
BBC 194–5, 204, 218, 234
Beckham, David 138–40, 149
Beijing Olympic Games (2008) 73, 76, 82, 112, 203, 215
    and JF's injury 84, 88, 92, 94, 109, 209
    UK Athletics performance at 103, 234

Belova, Irina 123
Berlin World Championships (2009) 89, 108–17
Birmingham 62, 122, 195–7
Bislett Stadium, Oslo 192–3
Black, Neil 80, 82, 83
Blonska, Lyudmila 49, 65–6, 74–5, 85, 93–4
Bolt, Usain 41, 116, 159–60, 193
BP 193
Brice, Paul (Bricey) 102, 105–6, 155, 163, 201–2
British Airways 193
British Olympic Association 237
Bull, Andy 23, 26

Caine, Andy 185
Campbell, Darren 164
Carruthers, Danielle 177, 183
Charlotte 16, 23, 24, 25–6, 33, 43, 202, 238
Chernova, Tatyana 4, 85, 112, 114, 125, 130

Götzis (2012) 191, 192
Olympic Games (2012) 214–15, 218, 221–2, 224–30, 235
World Championships (2011) 160–6
World Indoor Championships (2012) 179, 182
Child, Eilidh 206
Christie, Linford 129
City of Sheffield Athletics Club 25
Clarke, Lawrence 205
Club Quinta da Ria, Portugal 201–6
Coe, Sebastian 235–6
Collins, Dave 81, 87, 103–4
Commenee, Charles van 123–4, 178
    and Kelly Sotherton 45, 104
    and Phillips Idowu 207
    as UK Athletics director 104, 129, 130, 205
Commonwealth Games: Delhi (2010) 137–8
    Melbourne (2006) 50–2, 60
Cotgreave, Rick 25
Cowmeadow, Jane 99–100, 103, 109, 138
cryotherapy 145

Daegu World Championships (2011) 159–67, 182, 226, 230, 236
    run up to 146–8, 154, 157
Daley, Tom 176
Dannhauser, Mark 194
Delhi 137–8
Dennison, Kate 206, 223
Desenzano del Garda 103, 106–9
Diamond League events 192–3
Dijkstra, Paul 82–3
Dobrynska, Nataliya 4, 93, 122, 148, 191

Europeans (2010) 130, 131–2
Olympic Games (2012) 216, 218, 220, 222, 226
World Championships (2009) 112–16
World Championships (2011) 160, 161, 162
World Indoor Championships (2012) 179–82
Doha World Indoor Championships (2010) 122–3
Don Valley Stadium, Sheffield 18, 21–4, 26, 43
Douglas, Nathan 84
drugs doping and testing 93, 66–9, 125, 220

East Carolina University 42
Eddie 15, 16, 21, 34
800 metres 103, 115, 165–6, 227–9, 233, 247
English Institute of Sport (EIS) 62, 111, 126, 174
English Schools Championships 28–30, 32–3
Ennis, Carmel (JE's sister) 11–12, 26, 34, 142, 159, 160
    relationship with JE 12, 41–2, 87
    and sport 21, 22, 25
    watching events 115, 116, 117, 132, 236
Ennis, Jessica: childhood 8–9, 11–16
    school 16–18, 22–5, 43
    bullying 17–18, 24
    early interest in athletics 21–3, 26, 31–2, 47
    training with Chell 27–8, 31–3, 40, 42–3, 47, 51, 68, 77–8, 104, 113

early championships 28–30,
    39–41
Sheffield University 43–6, 50,
    62
injuries 30–1, 79–95, 100,
    104–6, 121–2, 125–8,
    144–5, 161–3
lottery funding 40, 176
appearance 47, 51–2, 117
and Andy Hill 43, 62, 142–3,
    238
relationship with Chell 57–61,
    64, 65, 75–6, 100, 102,
    172–3, 195
Europeans captaincy 128–30
build up to Olympics (2012)
    143, 153–8, 171, 173–6,
    182–3, 193–7, 201–9
as 'Face of the Games' 3, 171–2,
    205, 206
fame 137–8, 175, 241
sponsorship 138–42, 145,
    158–9, 172, 176, 193–5
Madame Tussauds 148–9
MBE 148
'Fatgate' 185, 189–91, 205
shoes 193–4
aftermath of Olympics (2012)
    233–42
see also individual championships
Ennis, Vinnie (JE's father) 9, 26, 42,
    142–3, 175
JE's childhood 10–11, 13–16,
    23, 30–1, 33, 34
JE's injuries 85, 94–5
JE's training 32, 60
Olympic Games (2012) 225,
    234, 237
watching events 109–10,
    114–16, 119, 132

European Championships: Barcelona
    (2010) 125–6, 128–32
    Gothenburg (2006) 61, 104
European Indoor Championships:
    Birmingham (2007) 62
    Paris (2011) 143, 144
European Junior Championships
    (2005) 48–9

Farah, Mo 160, 173, 178, 228, 234
'Fatgate' 185, 189–91, 205
Felix, Allyson 236
Forgemasters 140
Fountain, Hyleas 79, 93, 122, 131
    Olympic Games (2012) 215,
        216, 217
    World Championships (2011)
        160, 161
Freeman, Cathy 204

Götzis Hypo-Meeting: 2008 73,
    76–81, 85
    2010 124–5
    2011 146–8
    2012 176, 185, 190–2, 219,
        222, 230
Gautier, Nicola 26–7, 39, 193
Gay, Tyson 145–6
Georgina 34, 43
GQ 142
Great City Games, Manchester
    (2011/2012) 146, 183–4
Greene, Dai 129, 205–6, 208, 228

Hannah 31, 44, 61–2, 124, 173–4
Harper, Dawn 183
Harry, Prince 208
Higgins, Richard 126
high jump 106, 112, 161, 180,
    216–18

Hill, Andy 109, 114, 117, 126
    aftermath of Olympics 238,
        239, 241
    injury 86–7
    and JE's fame 133, 138, 141,
        171
    and JE's injuries 82, 88, 91–2
    Olympic Games (2012) 182,
        183, 185, 201, 225, 236
    relationship with JE 23–4, 43,
        45, 62, 142–3, 238
Hill, Matt 183
Hill, Mick 75, 90, 101, 157, 178
    Olympic Games (2012) 226, 227
Hollman, Julie 50
Holmes, Kelly 40, 90
Holmes, Mike 217–18, 227
hurdles 156, 177, 192–3, 203, 247
    Great City Games 184
    IAAF World Combined Events
        Challenge (2009) 107
    Olympic Games (2012) 143–4,
        214–15, 216, 218–19,
        237–8
    World Championships (2011)
        159, 160
    World Championships (2012)
        179–80
Hypo-Meeting, Götzis: 2008 73,
    76–7, 78–81, 85
    2010 124–5
    2011 146–8
    2012 176, 185, 190–2, 219,
        222, 230

IAAF (International Association of
    Athletics Federations) 66–8
IAAF World Combined Events
    Challenge, Desenzano del Garda
    (2009) 103, 106–9

Idowu, Phillips 207
Ingham, Steve 103, 111
International Association of Athletics
    Federations (IAAF) 66–8
Istanbul World Indoor
    Championships (2012) 176–7,
    178–82
Izmir, Turkey 49

Jaguar 193
javelin 101–2, 154, 163–4, 177–8,
    226–7, 247
John (decathlete) 107, 113, 131
Johnson, Michael 204, 228
Johnson-Thompson, Katarina (Kat) 53,
    196, 206, 214, 219, 221–2, 226
Jones, Lolo 122, 192, 203
Jones, Phil 64, 218, 234
Joshua, Anthony 238, 240

King Ecgbert School, Dore 22–3, 25,
    43
Klüft, Carolina 50, 61–4, 74, 75, 122,
    123

Lewis, Denise 52, 125, 132, 147,
    191–2, 228
Lindsay, Pete 102, 157
London Olympic Games (2012) 3–4,
    7, 143, 213–30, 233–7
    parade 240
    run up to 158, 175, 182–3,
        193–7, 201–9
long jump 104–6, 155, 197, 201–2,
    223–6, 247
Lorna 16, 22, 27, 238
Los Angeles 138–40

McCain Indoor City Challenge
    (2012) 176

McCain Inter City Cup Final, Cardiff
(2009) 106
Madame Tussauds 148–9
Manchester Great City Games (2012)
146, 183–4
Marie Claire 141
Middleton, Kate 207–8
Minichiello, Toni (Chell) 123
coaching JE 27–9, 31–3, 40,
42–3, 47, 51, 68, 77–8,
104, 110, 124, 153–6
'Fatgate' 189–91
JE's engagement 143
JE's injuries 81, 83, 85, 90, 121,
145, 146, 162
London Olympics (2012)
training 143, 171–5, 185,
194–7, 201, 217, 220–1
London Olympics (2012) 220,
222, 224–5, 227, 233,
235
long jump 104–6
media interviews 146, 147,
166 7
relationship with JE 57–61, 64,
65, 75–6, 100, 102, 172–3,
195
World Championships (2011)
165, 166–7
Myla 117, 124, 138, 153

National Lottery 40, 176
Northern Athletics Indoor
Championships (2011) 143
Northern Athletics Senior Indoor
Championships (2009) 106
Northern Championships, Sheffield
(2012) 176
Northern League Northern Premier
Division 49–50

Ohuruogu, Christine 69, 103
Olay 193
Olympic Games: Athens (2004) 50, 90
Beijing (2008) 73, 76, 82, 88,
92, 112, 203, 209, 215, 234
London (2012) 3–4, 7, 143,
158, 175, 183, 193–7,
201–9, 213 37
Olympic Medical Institute 82
Olympic Stadium, London 208, 209,
213–30, 233–7
Olympic Village, London 206, 207–9,
237
Omega 193, 238
Osaka World Championships (2007)
125
Ostapchuk, Nadzeya 220
Owens, Jesse 110

Paralympics 239
Peace Gardens, Sheffield 43, 238
Pearson, Sally 192, 193
Pistorius, Oscar 162
Pizza Hut 44
Porter, Tiffany 159, 178–9, 192
Portugal, Monte Gordo 201–6
Powell, Alison (JE's mother) 9, 28,
63, 142, 160, 195
JE at Aviva Startrack 18, 21
JE's childhood 10–11, 13–16,
30–1, 34
JE's injuries 85–6, 87
Olympic Games (2012) 204,
209, 222, 225, 234, 237
watching events 109–10, 115,
116, 118, 132
Powell, Rod 23, 33–4, 81–2, 109,
143, 177, 202
Powerade 158–9, 193
psychology of sports 45–6, 59

Radcliffe, Paula 81, 84, 104
Rafferty, Joe 118
Ribbans, Bill 89
Richards-Ross, Sanya 128
Rogers, Malcolm 25
Rose, Ali 40, 100–1, 109, 111, 154
    JE's calf injury 144, 145
    JE's foot injury 89, 90–1
    Olympic Games (2012) 222
Rutherford, Greg 205, 208, 234

Sanders, Nicola 62, 201–3, 205, 206, 207
Sayers, Goldie 129–30, 206, 207
Schippers, Dafne 221–2
Schwarzkopf, Lilli 229–30, 233, 235
Sharrow Junior School 16–17
Sheffield, reception for JE 43, 239
Sheffield City Council 118
Sheffield University 43, 44, 45–6, 50, 62
shot put 106, 113–14, 154, 219–20, 247
Skujyte, Austra 180, 181, 222, 226, 227
Sotherton, Kelly 50, 62, 63, 64, 85
    and Blonska 65–6, 74, 92–4
    calls JE Tadpole 51–3, 75–6
    and Charles van Commenee 45, 104
    Commonwealth Games 50
    Great City Games 184–5
sponsorship 193–5
Stedman, Suzi 103
Stylist 141
Suter, Derry 78, 83, 101, 145
    Olympic Games (2008) 90
    Olympic Games (2012) 213, 222, 233–4

Team Ennis 100–3, 213, 238
Team GB 201, 208, 237
Thompson, Mick 23, 24, 26
The Times 175
200 metres 80, 114, 162, 178, 220–1, 247

UK Athletics 81, 82, 87, 104, 144, 203–4
    'Fatgate' 189–91
    staff changes 111

Vogue 140–1

Whitehead, Richard 240
William, Prince 207–8
World Championships: Berlin (2009) 89, 108, 109–17
    Daegu (2011) 146, 147, 154, 157, 159–67, 182, 226, 230, 236
    Osaka (2007) 53, 61–4, 66, 69, 74, 93, 125
World Indoor Championships: Doha (2010) 122–3
    Istanbul (2012) 176–7, 178–82
World Junior Championships (2004) 41, 48
World Student Games (2005) 49
World Youth Championships (2003) 40–1

Yosypenko, Lyudmyla 227

Zelinka, Jessica 79, 147
    Olympic Games (2012) 204–5, 215, 216, 222, 229–30, 233
    World Championships (2011) 160